Portraits of Mexican Americans

Pathfinders in the Mexican American Communities

by
Dr. Theresa Pérez

with
Nancy Márquez
Martina Granados
Lynette Zerounian

illustrated by Jim Márquez

Cover by Jim Márquez

Copyright © Good Apple, 1991

ISBN No. 0-86653-605-1

Printing No. 987654321

GOOD APPLE
1204 BUCHANAN ST., BOX 299
CARTHAGE, IL 62321-0299

S I M O N & S C H U S T E R *A Paramount Communications Company*

TABLE OF CONTENTS

GA1324

DEDICATION

This book is dedicated to little Gilbert Saiz
who would have enjoyed reading it.

To the Mexican Americans
whose contributions are chronicled in its pages.

To the children who will read it
to gain a better understanding of Mexican Americans

INTRODUCTION

The history of the United States is incomplete without the inclusion of the story of Mexican Americans. Mexican Americans are often called the forgotten people because of their lack of inclusion in history books. When they are included, they are often portrayed in either a negative light or as a caricature or stereotype, which only adds to the lack of understanding about Mexican Americans.

Mexican Americans represent a very large and important part of our society and they are not newcomers. Even when they are grouped together with other "Hispanics," they make up the largest number. Most of them live in the Southwest for historical reasons, many have been there for centuries even before the Anglo-Americans, some migrated during the Mexican Revolution of 1910 and others are still making their way into the United States because of the availability of work that is not present in their country. They go by many names depending upon their region or their politics: Mexicans, Mexican Americans, Hispanics, Chicanos, Californios, Tejanos and Manitos are but a few of the names, but they are basically the same people with a common language or culture that binds them.

They have added to and enriched our society through their many contributions. Among these contributions are their willingness to work hard and harvest the crops in the valleys of the Southwest as well as in other parts of the country, thereby making these valleys among the richest in the world. Their early knowledge of how to use the land, the minerals and the animals of the Southwest, shared with others, has added greatly to the development of the region. Mexican Americans have also given us their finest and most visionary men and women for politics, government, education and scholarship, as authors, writers, artists and in many other fields. This book touches only on a few of the achievements and contributions of Mexican Americans. They deserve to be recognized.

GA1324

TO THE TEACHER

COOPERATIVE LEARNING

Many of the activities in this book are designed to stimulate thoughtful and lively interaction in small groups. We recommend that the small groups consist of no more than four or five students for better group interaction, that teachers make the tasks clear to the students before making the assignment, and then that they let the groups assume responsibility for their own interaction. A good role for the teacher during small group activities is that of developing challenging questions to stimulate students' thinking.

If each student is given a role to play in the small group such as reporter, group harmonizer, facilitator and timekeeper (teachers can make up the roles and functions), and it is clear to the students what these roles stand for, the small groups will probably function better. Two rules that teachers may want to promote in the small groups are everyone has the responsibility to ask for help if he needs it and that only one person from each group may approach the teacher to ask a question, and this only after the group has determined that they cannot find the answer among themselves. This will enhance the management of the small groups.

Finally at the end of the small group activity or group discussion, each group or each reporter should be asked to report on the findings of their group. This presents a wonderful opportunity for task enrichment, whole class interaction and for providing feedback to all the children.

SPANISH LANGUAGE ACTIVITIES

As an extra learning experience for students using this book, many exercises promote a "figure out" approach to dealing with written Spanish and offer the opportunity for introducing Spanish as a second language to students, or for reinforcing skills the Spanish-speaking students already possess.

As a guide for teachers and students who do not speak Spanish, pronunciation keys are provided on each page for Spanish names and words that are introduced. These are approximate pronunciations for Spanish and the underlined syllables should be stressed.

GA1324

THE CALIFORNIA MISSIONS

Have you ever traveled on Highway 1 along the California coast?
What beauty!
This is the old route of the Spaniards in settling California with missions.
Visit as many of the missions as you can.

In the state of California there are twenty-one missions from SAN DIEGO to SONOMA. In 1769 Father JUNIPERO SERRA, a Franciscan priest, founded the first mission in the chain of missions beginning in San Diego. This is how the era of the mission began in California. From San Diego he traveled to MONTEREY and founded the mission of SAN CARLOS. Father Serra founded nine missions, and his successor, Father LAUSEN, founded another nine.

The missions were the first schools for the native people of California. Here they learned to read and write. The missions also served as technical schools.

The Spanish, who ruled Mexico at the time, established the missions and erected PRESIDIOS, or military posts, to protect their large ships that traveled from Mexico to the Philippines. They needed to protect and service their ships on the return trip to Mexico, and northern California was the first land sighted. The misiones, the presidios and the PUEBLOS (towns) that sprang up next to the missions helped to settle the Southwest.

The missions controlled large blocks of land and became very self-sufficient, growing their own food supplies. Among the crops that the priests introduced to California were peaches, strawberries, almonds, olives, figs, oranges, lemons, grapes, apples, pears, plums, chives, pomegranates, walnuts, apricots, limes and raspberries. The Spanish also introduced wheat and alfalfa. California continues to produce these crops in great abundance.

Before the founding of the missions, the Indians already grew corn, beans and melons. They also knew how to use water in the desert to make things grow. Having learned from the Indians and the Spaniards, the men who came to the Southwest from Mexico were also good farmers. They introduced plows, hoes and spades and brought fruit trees and plants that grew well in the desert soil.

The missions prospered and operated many large ranches. In 1834 Mission SAN GABRIEL operated seventeen large ranches, owned 105,000 head of cattle, 20,000 horses and 40,000 sheep. Many thousands of Indians lived and worked on these ranches which were worth $78,000,000. These early missions established the pattern California agriculture uses today.

LA MISION (lah   mee-see-on)
SAN DIEGO (sahn   dee-ay-go)
SONOMA (so-no-ma)
JUNIPERO SERRA (hoo-nee-pay-ro   ser-rah)
MONTEREY (mon-ter-ray)

SAN CARLOS (sahn   car-los)
LAUSEN (lah-oo-sen)
PRESIDIOS (pray-see-dee-os)
PUEBLOS (poo-ay-blohs)
SAN GABRIEL (sahn   gay-bree-el)

GA1324

EL CAMINO REAL
Transportation

Roads have many uses and are important for travel and transporting goods and services to cities and towns. The native peoples of the Southwest developed many early roads or trails before the coming of the Spaniards. Later, these trails were used by both Spaniards and Mexicans to build their roads. Many of these original trails are still in use today as railroads and highways.

One of the earliest highways was known as EL CAMINO REAL, the Royal Highway. These roads connected settlements within California, New Mexico and Texas. In California, El Camino Real linked the twenty-one missions and became the scenic Highway 1 of California today.

Trace El Camino Real from the Mexican border to northern California by connecting the places where missions were established. On a map of California, find the present day location of each of the missions.

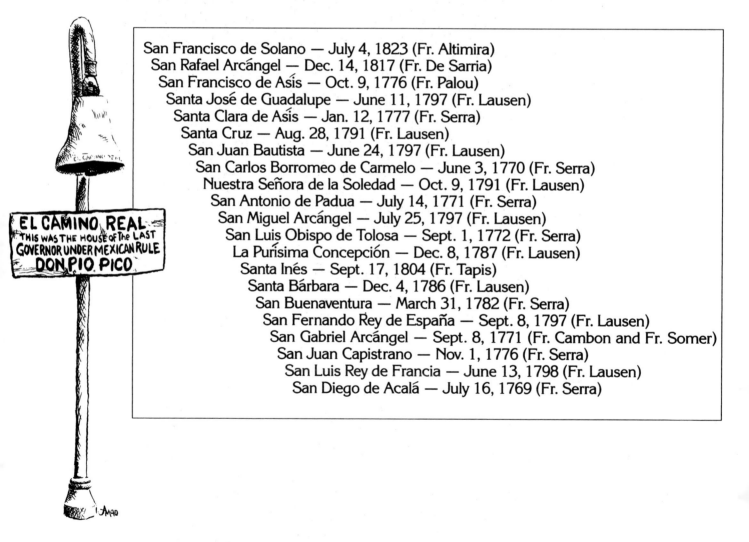

San Francisco de Solano — July 4, 1823 (Fr. Altimira)
San Rafael Arcángel — Dec. 14, 1817 (Fr. De Sarria)
San Francisco de Asís — Oct. 9, 1776 (Fr. Palou)
Santa José de Guadalupe — June 11, 1797 (Fr. Lausen)
Santa Clara de Asís — Jan. 12, 1777 (Fr. Serra)
Santa Cruz — Aug. 28, 1791 (Fr. Lausen)
San Juan Bautista — June 24, 1797 (Fr. Lausen)
San Carlos Borromeo de Carmelo — June 3, 1770 (Fr. Serra)
Nuestra Señora de la Soledad — Oct. 9, 1791 (Fr. Lausen)
San Antonio de Padua — July 14, 1771 (Fr. Serra)
San Miguel Arcángel — July 25, 1797 (Fr. Lausen)
San Luis Obispo de Tolosa — Sept. 1, 1772 (Fr. Serra)
La Purísima Concepción — Dec. 8, 1787 (Fr. Lausen)
Santa Inés — Sept. 17, 1804 (Fr. Tapis)
Santa Bárbara — Dec. 4, 1786 (Fr. Lausen)
San Buenaventura — March 31, 1782 (Fr. Serra)
San Fernando Rey de España — Sept. 8, 1797 (Fr. Lausen)
San Gabriel Arcángel — Sept. 8, 1771 (Fr. Cambon and Fr. Somer)
San Juan Capistrano — Nov. 1, 1776 (Fr. Serra)
San Luis Rey de Francia — June 13, 1798 (Fr. Lausen)
San Diego de Acalá — July 16, 1769 (Fr. Serra)

EL CAMINO REAL (el cah·mee·no ray·ahl)

2

GA1324

54 YEARS AND 600 MILES OF MISSIONS

Write the name and the year for each of the missions founded on the lines below, putting them in chronological order, from the first mission founded to the last.

ORDER	NAME	YEAR	WORLD EVENTS
first	_____	_____	
second	_____	_____	
third	_____	_____	
fourth	_____	_____	
fifth	_____	_____	
sixth	_____	_____	Declaration of Independence
seventh	_____	_____	
eighth	_____	_____	Cornwallis
ninth	_____	_____	Preliminary Peace Treaty in Paris
tenth	_____	_____	
eleventh	_____	_____	U.S. Constitution
twelfth	_____	_____	
thirteenth	_____	_____	
fourteenth	_____	_____	
fifteenth	_____	_____	
sixteenth	_____	_____	
seventeenth	_____	_____	
eighteenth	_____	_____	Napoleon Bonaparte
nineteenth	_____	_____	Grito de Dolores, Sept. 16th
twentieth	_____	_____	Monroe President
twenty-first	_____	_____	Agustín Iturbe I of Mexico

CALIFORNIA'S SCENIC HIGHWAY 1

1. Have you ever traveled on Highway 1 along the California coast?

2. What beauty!

3. This is the old route of the Spaniards in settling California with missions.

4. Visit as many of the missions as you can.

The beginning sentences of the story of the missions illustrate four kinds of sentences. Write the number of the sentence which is described below.

_____ DECLARATIVE sentence makes a statement.

_____ INTERROGATIVE sentence asks a question.

_____ EXCLAMATORY sentence makes a surprising or strong statement.

_____ IMPERATIVE sentence gives a command or direction.

All of the other sentences in the reading are _____.

Pick five sentences from the reading and change the declarative sentences to the interrogative form.

_____

_____

_____

_____

_____

GA1324

CALIFORNIO

PIO PICO
Last Mexican Governor
of California
1801-1894

When people are asked to name some of the Spanish and Mexican governors of California, it is often a surprise to them to find out that in 1768, eight years before the Declaration of Independence of the United States, California already had an established government.

One of the most interesting native Californian governors was PIO PICO. Born in 1801, when California was under Spanish rule, he lived almost a century, through many changes that marked the history of Mexico and the United States.

In 1845 Pio Pico led a group of rebels against Governor MANUEL MICHELTOREÑA and defeated him at Los Angeles, becoming governor of ALTA CALIFORNIA, the present day state of California. In May of 1846 the United States declared war against Mexico, which ended with Mexico's defeat and the TREATY OF GUADALUPE HIDALGO. As a result of this treaty, Mexico lost half of its territory to the United States, including California. The last battle of the war was fought on Pico's ranch.

During the times of the Mexican governors, Governor Pio Pico amassed considerable wealth and land holdings. The Mexican government owed Governor Pico a great sum of money, which he tried to collect in Mexico after the U.S. took over California. When he returned to Los Angeles in 1848, a new history of California was beginning.

In the second part of his life, Governor Pico became a model citizen, using his wealth and influence to promote civic interests, education, banking and town development. He was elected to the Los Angeles City Council and became a pioneer in the first oil venture in California. His mansion and his name on streets and towns in Los Angeles are constant reminders of his life.

Governor Pio Pico was one of many Californios who lived and prospered long before this part of the country became a part of the United States.

Pico died in 1894 at the age of 93. He is still remembered by those who read his autobiography dictated to a friend at the age of 77 as a kind and courteous man. In his memoirs he related the time when he borrowed $62,000 from an Anglo friend, using his ranch as collateral. The ranch was valued at $200,000. When he returned two months later to pay back the money, he was told that he had sold the ranch for $62,000. The courts upheld the swindle.

Governor Pico's life represents the history of California during the nineteenth century, which resulted in the loss of land and fortunes for many people.

CALIFORNIO (cah-lee-for-nee-o)
PIO PICO (pee-o pee-co)
MANUEL MICHELTOREÑA (mahn-oo-el mee-chehl-tor-ey-nah)
ALTA CALIFORNIA (ahl-tah cah-lee-for-nee-ah)
GUADALUPE HIDALGO (goo-ah-dah-loo-pay ee-dahl-go)

GA1324

GOVERNORS OF CALIFORNIA

Below is a list of the governors of Alto California, under Spanish and Mexican rule. The Spanish governors, and many of the Mexican ones, were more like military rulers.

Los Gobernadores Españoles de California

1.	Gaspar de Portolá	1769-1770
2.	Felipe de Barri	1770-1775
3.	Felipe de Neve	1775-1782
4.	Pedro Fages	1782-1791
5.	José Antonio Romeu	1791-1792
6.	José Joaquín de Arrillaga	1792-1794
7.	Diego de Borica	1794-1800
8.	José Joaquín de Arrillaga	1800-1814
9.	José Argüello	1814-1815
10.	Pablo Vicente Sola	1815-1821

Los Gobernadores Mexicanos de California

1.	Pablo Vicente Sola	1821-1822
2.	Luis Argüello	1822-1825
3.	José Maria de Echeandía	1825-1831
4.	Manuel Victoria	1831-1831
5.	José María de Echeandía	1831-1833
6.	José Figueroa	1833-1835
7.	José Castro	1835-1836
8.	Nicolás Gutiérrez	1836-1836
9.	Mariano Chico	1836-1836
10.	Nicolás Gutiérrez	1836-1836
11.	Juan Bautista Alvardo	1836-1842
12.	Manuel Micheltoreña	1842-1845
13.	Pio Pico	1845-1846

EL CAMINO REAL
THIS WAS THE HOUSE OF THE LAST GOVERNOR UNDER MEXICAN RULE
DON PIO PICO

FOR DISCUSSION:

1. Which Spanish governor was in office the longest? _____

2. Which Spanish governors were in office two years or less? _____

_____

3. Which Mexican governor was in office the longest? _____

4. Which Mexican governors were in office two years or less? _____

_____

5. Which person was governor under both Spanish and Mexican rule? _____

6. What does ALTA CALIFORNIA mean? _____

7. What other California is there? _____

8. Who was the last Mexican governor of California? _____

Can you list the governors of California after the United States took possession of Alta California?

GA1324

SPANISH NAMES IN THE SOUTHWEST

Pio Pico and many other Mexicans and Spaniards left their names and the names of saints, towns and descriptive Spanish words on many places in the Southwest.

Find a map of the United States and locate the states of the Southwest. The name of each of these states is based on a Spanish word. Use a dictionary to find the meaning of each.

CALIFORNIA _____

TEXAS _____

NEW MEXICO _____

ARIZONA _____

COLORADO _____

In groups of four or five, have each group examine a map of one of these states. Make a list for each state and the cities on the map which have names of Spanish origin.

State _____

Cities with Spanish names:

If you live in a city in one of the states of the Southwest, examine a street map of your city to find out how many streets have names of Spanish origin.

GA1324

TRATADO

TREATY OF GUADALUPE HIDALGO

In February 1848, the United States and Mexico signed the Treaty of GUADALUPE HIDALGO that ended the war between Mexico and the United States. The war with Mexico began in 1846 over a boundary dispute in Texas. By the Treaty of Guadalupe Hidalgo, Mexico surrendered one half of its territory to the United States.

Among the rights given to the Mexicans under the treaty was the right to retain their property and the right to their language, culture and customs. The treaty also gave the Mexican residents the choice of becoming citizens of the United States or returning to Mexico. The Mexicans, most of whom were native born and whose families had never lived anywhere else, elected to stay in the Southwest. These people were the first Mexican Americans.

After the Treaty of Guadalupe Hidalgo, things changed dramatically in the Southwest. English became the official language as courts conducted business in English and almost all of the laws were written in English. The Anglo-Americans established laws to protect their interests. Although they were born in this land, Mexicans, Indians and Chinese were considered foreigners.

Ordinances were passed to outlaw Mexican FIESTAS. It was against the law to testify in Spanish. Most teachers spoke only English. The use of Spanish was forbidden in most schools. The Mexican Americans knew little or no English, and with the changes in the laws it was not long before they began to lose their land, cattle and way of life.

Land passed into the hands of the Anglo-Americans in a variety of ways. Some of these ways were legal manueverings and some not so legal. Landowners were sometimes tricked out of their land, or even murdered. In northern California, Anglo-Americans took the land by "squatting" on it, which meant living on it without paying for it and refusing to get off. Mexican Americans also lost their land through legal court battles, high attorney fees and a lack of knowledge of both the English language and the United States laws. As if this were not enough, they could not pay their taxes because of poor economic conditions caused by drought and floods.

In Texas, where the economy depended on cattle ranching, wealth was measured by the number of cattle and other animals on the land. As in the rest of the Southwest, Texans also lost their land in costly court battles and had to work as laborers. As cotton became more important, they labored in cotton camps. The Mexican Americans in the Southwest entered a difficult period. They began to experience more discrimination with segregated schools, restaurants and cemeteries. It has been said that they became "strangers in their own land."

TRATADO (trah-tah-do)
GUADALUPE HIDALGO (goo-ah-dah-loo-pay ee-dahl-go)
FIESTAS (fee-ess-tahs)

8

GA1324

TREATIES AND RIGHTS

Look up more about the Mexican American War and the Treaty of Guadalupe Hidalgo in your library.

1. What is a treaty?

2. Why do they call this treaty the Treaty of Guadalupe Hidalgo?

3. Who were the presidents of Mexico and the United States when this treaty was signed?

Discuss and debate in groups:

1. What happens when a treaty is broken?

2. Is the Treaty of Guadalupe Hidalgo still in effect?

3. What rights do people have to keep and use Spanish in the United States?

4. When Spanish-speaking people can't understand English, what responsibility does the government have to reach them?

5. What kind of things would you be able to do if you knew Spanish, that you couldn't do if you didn't know it?

GA1324

ARTICLE VIII
Treaty of Guadalupe Hidalgo

ESPAÑOL:

ARTICULO VIII

Los Mexicanos establecidos hoy en territorios pertenecientes antes a México y que quedan para lo futuro dentro de los límites señalados por el presente tratado a los Estados Unidos, podrán permanecer en donde ahora habitan, o trasladarán en cualquier tiempo a la República Mexicana, conservando en los indicados territorios los bienes que poseen, o enagenándolos y pasando su valor a donde les convenga, sin que por esto pueda exigírseles ningún género de contribución, gravamen o impuesto.

Los que prefieran permanecer en los indicados territorios podrán conservar el título y derechos de ciudadanía de los Estados Unidos. Mas la elección entre una y otra ciudadanía, deberán hacerla dentro de un año contado desde la fecha del cange de las ratificaciones de este tratado. Y los que permanecieren en los indicados territorios después del trans-currido del año, sin haber declarado su intención de retener el carácter de mexicanos, le considerará que han elegido ser ciudadanos de los Estados Unidos.

Las propiedades de todo género exis-tentes en los expresados teritorios, y que pertenecen ahora a Mexicanos no establecidos en ellas, serán respetadas inviolablemente. Sus actuales dueños, los herederos de éstos, y los Mexicanos que en lo venidero puedan adquirir por contrato las indicadas propiedades, disfrutarán respeto de ellas tan amplia garantía, como si perteneciesen a ciudadanos de los Estados Unidos.

ENGLISH:

ARTICLE VIII

Mexicans now established in territories previously belonging to Mexico, and which remain for the future within the limits of the United States, as defined by the present treaty, shall be free to continue where they now reside, or to remove at any time to the Mexican Republic, retaining the property by which they possess in the said territories, or disposing thereof, and removing the proceeds wherever they please, without their being subjected, on this account, to any contribution, tax or charge whatever.

Those who shall prefer to remain in the said territories, may either retain the title and rights of Mexican citizens, or acquire, those of citizens of the United States. But they shall be under the obligation to make their election within one year from the date of the exchange of ratification of this treaty; and those who shall remain in the said territories after the expiration of that year, without having declared their intention to retain the character of Mexicans, shall be consid-ered to have elected to become citizens of the United States.

In the said territories, property of every kind, now belonging to Mexicans not established there, shall be inviolably respected. The present owner, the heirs of these, and all Mexicans who may hereafter acquire said property by contract, shall enjoy with respect to it guaranties equally ample as if this same belonged to citizens of the United States.

GA1324

EL TRATADO
(the treaty)

Read the English version of Article VIII of the Treaty of Guadalupe Hidalgo and discuss its wording and meaning. It was written in 1848, so the handwriting and the wording may be different. Also, notice that the treaty, EL TRATADO, was written in both Spanish and in English, side by side. Below is an example from a copy of the original document.

Artículo VIII.

Los Mexicanos establecidos hoy en territorios pertenecientes antes á México y que quedan para lo futuro dentro de los límites señalados por el presente tratado á los Estados Unidos, podrán permanecer en donde ahora habitan; ó trasladarse en cualquier

Article VIII.

Mexicans now established in territories previously belonging to Mexico, and which remain for the future within the limits of the United States, as defined by the present treaty, shall be free to continue where they now reside, or to remove at any time to the Mexican

After you have read the English version, try to find the words in the Spanish version which translate the following:

the United States _____

article _____

the Mexican Republic _____

territories _____

the title and rights _____

within one year _____

citizens _____

property _____

_____

EL TRATADO (el   trah-<u>tah</u>-do)

11

MEXICO'S TERRITORY

Mexico was once larger than it is today and covered parts of what is now the United States. On the maps for each of the following years, color the part that belonged to Mexico.

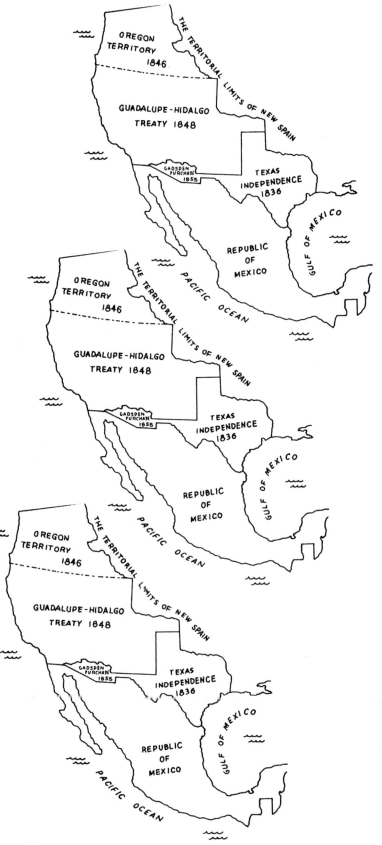

1810
Spain had control of what is today Mexico and parts of the Southwest. It was called Nueva Espana, or New Spain.

1822
Mexico gained its independence from Spain and all the territories belonged to Mexico.

1836
Texas claimed and won its independence from Mexico.

1846

The part known as the Oregon Territory was lost.

1848

As a result of the U.S.-Mexico War, Mexico gave up areas which now form the states of California, Arizona, Utah, Nevada and parts of Colorado and New Mexico.

1853

The Gadsden Purchase, made by James Gadsden on behalf of the U.S. government, renegotiated the boundaries set by the Treaty of Guadalupe Hidalgo and gave another small section to the United States.

COOPERATIVE PROJECT:

In groups of four or five, investigate one of the years and events described above and on the preceding page, and find out more about what happened.

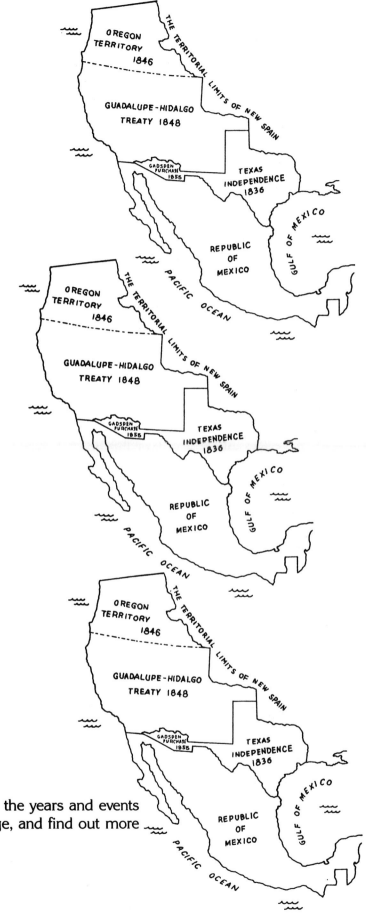

GA1324

LA TIERRA
The Story of the Land

The Southwest was always considered a frontier by Spain and Mexico. It was sparsely populated and only the hardiest of citizens lived in such surroundings. As a result, a way of life that depended on the large RANCHOS (ranches) and the need for large tracts of land developed in the Southwest. With such a small population it was possible to give away large tracts of land for people to settle. The ranchos were successful and self-sufficient, and it was a peaceful life. The Spaniards and Indians learned from each other and produced this new way of life. They married and their children became the MESTIZOS, or first Mexicans. The Spanish kings gave large tracts of land to their deserving subjects. Sargeant PERALTA, a Mestizo soldier, was given the land that is now Oakland, Alameda and Berkeley in California. The missions operated by the PADRES also received much land.

The custom of giving large amounts of land continued after 1821, when Spain lost the Southwest to Mexico. In 1834 Mexico gave the mission lands to people in the form of land grants. Between 1833 and 1846 the Mexican government gave away 400 land grants that were between 4000 and 300,000 acres. By 1848, 800 ranchos had 8 million acres of land in California.

After California became a state, the United States government gave California nearly 11 million acres of land. Real estate agents could buy the land for very little money and, again, the land fell into the hands of just a few people. By 1871, 516 men owned over 8½ million acres of land. Two men by the names of Miller and Lux, owned 2½ million acres of land. Railroad companies were also given railroad grants for building tracks. By 1871, the railroad companies owned 11 million acres of land. For example, large sections of California were given to the Southern Pacific Railroad, which it still owns.

TO THINK ABOUT:

Giving large amounts of land away when there is a small population seems like a good idea. What do you think happens when there is a big population and the land is in the hands of a few?

LA TIERRA (lah   tee-er-rah)
RANCHOS (rahn-chos)
MESTIZOS (mes-tee-sos)
PERALTA (pay-rahl-tah)
PADRES (pah-drays)

VAQUEROS

CATTLE

When you picture the Southwest, you might think of large herds of cattle. This type of scene is common, and it is easy for anyone to get the impression that the Southwest has always been that way. But before the coming of the Spaniards to this part of the country there were no cattle or domestic animals of any kind, except the dog.

Among the animals introduced by the Spaniards to the Southwest were horses, cattle, burros and hogs. The native peoples, called "Indians," had never seen a horse and at first they thought it was a big dog. The Spaniards also introduced the customs of branding livestock, the RODEO or roundup, and the herding of cattle by cowboys on horses.

The animals brought by the Spaniards could live in the desert. Longhorn cattle, originally from Africa, were well suited to the desert and to the Southwest, since many years before Arabs had introduced the animals from the desert to Spain.

The original horses were small and strong and could protect themselves from wild animals. These horses were called MESTEÑOS, and they could go without water for long distances. These mesteños later became the famous mustangs of the Southwest.

Many of these desert animals became separated from their original herds and grew wild. For example, the first few hundred herd of cattle left on their own began to multiply and soon became thousands. As time went by, people could own the wild cattle if they could round them up.

VAQUEROS (vah-kay-ros)
RODEO (ro-day-o)
MESTEÑOS (mes-tayn-yos)

GA1324

WILD AND DOMESTIC ANIMALS

In groups of four or five, talk about the differences between wild animals and domestic animals.

Name as many wild animals and domestic animals as you can in fifteen minutes. Choose a timekeeper and recorder for your group.

WILD ANIMALS	DOMESTIC ANIMALS
_____	_____
_____	_____
_____	_____
_____	_____
_____	_____
_____	_____
_____	_____
_____	_____
_____	_____
_____	_____
_____	_____
_____	_____

Collaborate with the other groups by combining the lists of domestic and wild animals. Each recorder will participate in creating the combined list.

STATISTICS:

Each group can calculate the percentage of wild animals they came up with, as compared to the combined list. Then calculate the percentage of domestic animals of the group, as compared to the combined total list.

Combined number of wild animals _____ Your group's number _____ _____%

Combined number of domestic animals _____ Your group's number _____ _____%

GA1324

ANIMALES

Some English and Spanish words appear very similar. Often the English word is "borrowed" from Spanish. Other times, both the Spanish and English words are derived from words in Latin, one of the sources of both the Spanish and English languages.

Here are some names of animals in Spanish. On the lines below, guess which one is a translation for each of the English words.

burro	animal	caballo
perro	gato	puerco
venado	pajaro	vibora
gallo	camello	chango

horse _____

camel _____

animal _____

deer _____

rooster _____

snake _____

cat _____

monkey _____

pig _____

bird _____

dog _____

burro _____

If there are some you are not sure of, look them up in an English-Spanish dictionary.

GA1324

LA REATA

VAQUEROS
Cowboys

The VAQUEROS, who herded cattle in the Southwest, were the first cowboys of the West. Most of the original vaqueros were mission Indians who had the difficult job of training the wild MESTEÑOS, or mustangs, and watching over the unfriendly longhorn cattle. The horses were also known as broncos, from the Spanish word BRONCO, which means "wild." At first the mission fathers refused to let the Indians ride the horses, but when the herds of cattle grew, the PADRES needed more help and taught the Indians to ride.

Many years later, when the Southwest was no longer a part of Spain or Mexico and the era of the mission RANCHOS was over, Americans copied the ways of the Mexican vaquero. They built ranchos and used ropes, saddles and spurs. Even the word *vaquero* was understood as "buckaroo."

The vaquero was an expert horseman who used la reata for roping cattle and capturing the wild mesteños. La reata, a rawhide rope, was a valuable tool for the vaquero who became a master roper. He spent many hours practicing with his sixty-foot rope until he could rope from his horse at full gallop or standing still. Later la reata became the lariat.

The vaquero's clothing was adapted for life on the range. He wore CHAPARRERAS, which were leather pants over his legs to keep the weeds, grasses and cactus off of him. The cowboys later called these chaparreras "chaps." Vaqueros also wore SOMBREROS to keep the hot desert sun and rain off of them. The SOMBRERO GALEONADO, or ten-gallon hat as it was later known, was also used to catch water for the rider and his horse to drink from in the desert. The big sombrero could also be used to wave in the air as a signal to other riders.

Another important article of clothing for the vaquero was his high-heeled boots. The reason for the heels on the boots was to keep the boot from sliding through the open stirrup. A vaquero would not want to get his foot caught in the stirrups while he was roping. It could mean his death.

The Mexican saddle was the vaquero's most prized possession. The vaquero would sell his horse before he would sell his saddle. Mexican craftsmen improved the Spanish saddle in ways that made it easier for the vaquero to do his work. By giving the saddle a fat horn in front to tie one end of the reata, it became easier to rope. Before this invention, the vaquero had to use the horse's tail to anchor the rope. The saddle also had ARMAS, or armor, to protect the vaquero from the horns of an angry bull. Roping and riding required a perfect saddle, and the Mexican saddle fit the vaquero like a glove. Today's western saddle looks very much like the saddle used by the vaquero.

LA REATA (lah ray-ah-tah)
VAQUEROS (vah-kay-ros)
MESTEÑOS (mes-tayn-yos)
BRONCO (bron-co)
PADRES (pah-drays)

RANCHOS (rahn-chos)
CHAPARRERAS (cha-pahr-ray-ras)
SOMBREROS (som-bray-ros)
SOMBRERO GALEONADO (som-bray-ro gah-lay-o-nah-do)
ARMAS (ar-mahs)

SPANISH IN THE SOUTHWEST

In the ranch country of the Southwest, many Spanish words were "borrowed" from the Mexican vaqueros and became part of our English vocabulary.

Here are some Spanish words that English has borrowed. Write the English word for each one and give a brief definition for the word. Use a Spanish-English dictionary if you find it necessary.

SPANISH	ENGLISH	DEFINITION
adobe		
adios		
alfalfa		
amigo		
arroyo		
bronco		
cañon		
chaparreras		
chile		
corral		
coyote		
fiesta		
gracias		
guitarra		
hacienda		
mesteño		
padre		
patio		
pinto		
plaza		
poncho		
pronto		
pueblo		
rodeo		
serape		
si		
siesta		
sombrero		
vaquero		

Circle the words that are spelled exactly the same in Spanish and English.

A STORY OF THE SOUTHWEST

Write a story about the Southwest and cowboys, using as many of the words borrowed from Spanish as you can.

_____
(title)

_____
_____
_____
_____
_____
_____
_____
_____
_____
_____
_____
_____
_____
_____
_____
_____
_____
_____
_____
_____
_____
_____
_____
_____
_____

Illustrate your story.

ORO

MINERS IN GOLD COUNTRY

How many times have you read that James Marshall discovered gold in California in 1848? Did you know that Mexicans were already mining gold along the coastal mountains between Santa Cruz and Los Angeles?

FRANCISCO LOPEZ, a Mexican, discovered gold on March 9, 1842. He was out riding his horse and became hungry, so he dug up some onions and noticed flakes of gold clinging to them.

In 1845, near San Jose, California, Captain ANDRES CASTILLERO, a Mexican officer, made another important discovery. He found the first quicksilver mine to be discovered in North America. Quicksilver is an important metal in removing gold and silver from ore. Many years before, another miner in PACHUCA, Mexico, discovered how to extract silver from ore by treating it with quicksilver.

After James Marshall's find in 1848, in an area not settled by Mexicans, thousands of people rushed to California from all over the world, seeking the precious metal. Most of these people, who are known as Forty-Niners, had little knowledge of mining and were forced to rely on the more experienced Mexican miners. Miners from SONORA, Mexico, whose ancestors had been mining since 1763, heard of the gold and moved their families to California to work the southern mines in central California. In 1849 gold was discovered by Mexicans in one of the largest towns, named Sonora, after their hometown in Mexico.

Mexican miners brought with them important skills they had developed, skills passed on to them for generations, since the time of the Spaniards. In the year 1549, ZACATECAS, a town in Mexico, became a roaring silver camp when a major silver strike was made. An important discovery made by the Spanish of the SANTA RITA mine in northern New Mexico added the development of copper mining techniques. Mexican miners also had practice in the important silver mining centers of DURANGO and CHIHUAHUA in northern Mexico. By 1600 Mexico produced more silver than any other country in the world. By the end of the 1700's Mexico had 3000 silver mines and a school of mines which was considered one of the most important scientific institutions for the study and improvement of mining methods in the world.

In California, Mexican miners introduced equipment and methods to sift gold from the rivers. They called this BATEA, and used a flat-bottom pan to wash gold from the sand of the streams. In places where there was no water, they used a dry panning method which removed the sand from the gold by tossing gold-ladened sand into the air and blowing on it. The lighter sand blew away and the heavier grains of gold dropped back into the pan. After a time when most of the gold was removed from the streams and had to be dug out of the mountains, the Mexicans introduced a stone wheel called an ARRASTRA. The wheel was drawn by a mule, or powered by a waterwheel that crushed the ore. The gold was then separated from the ore by combining it with quicksilver from the New ALMADEN mine near San Jose.

GA1324

Mexicans contributed to mining in still other ways. The Forty-Niners, having little experience with mining, looked to the legal system established by Spain and Mexico for setting up their mining laws. They used the Mexican law, which stated that property in mines depends on discovery and development. Later, when mining became big business, Mexican men were used as laborers. They were considered the best workers and essential in mining copper, which had become an important metal for electricity.

Even with all the contributions made by the Mexicans, they were not welcomed in the mines by the Forty-Niners and were often barred from digging where the Forty-Niners were in the majority. In 1850 a group of Mexican miners in Sonora, California, were forced off their claim by the Forty-Niners. They moved further north where they struck it rich, and again they were forced off the claim. This town was later known as Columbia, an important mining center in California.

Another way in which they were discriminated against was in having to pay a tax. Before a miner could stake a claim, he had to pay a $20 tax imposed on all foreign born. Usually all Mexicans had to pay even though they were American citizens. Later, when the tax became $30 a month, many miners could not pay. The average miner earned $3 to $4 a day and expenses were high. Items were brought from great distances, which made them cost more. Flour cost $1 a pound, pork $2 a pound, a can of peaches $10 and a pair of boots cost 6 ounces of gold.

The Forty-Niners were angry because they believed the "foreigners" were staking out the best claims. They also resented the Spanish language because they could not understand it. They didn't like Mexican amusements, like the FANDANGOS and bullfights, which seemed very strange to them. Although many Mexicans were natives of California and had a right to the gold, they were outnumbered and forced off the diggings by the Forty-Niners.

ORO (o-ro)
FRANCISCO LOPEZ (frahn-sees-co   loh-pes)
ANDRES CASTILLERO (ahn-drays   cahs-tee-yer-o)
PACHUCA (pah-choo-cah)
SONORA (so-nor-ah)
ZACATECAS (sah-cah-tay-cahs)
SANTA RITA (sahn-tah   ree-tah)

DURANGO (doo-rahn-go)
CHIHUAHUA (chee-oo-ah-oo-ah)
BATEA (bah-tay-ah)
ARRASTRA (ar-ras-trah)
ALMADEN (al-mah-den)
FANDANGOS (fan-dahn-gos)

22

LAWS

It has been said that we are a nation of laws.

Laws are rules that people live by.

In the early days of the Southwest, the Spanish and Mexicans introduced laws that governed the use of water, the idea of community property and the claims on mining rights.

The Spanish-Mexican irrigation law says that water is owned by everyone and not just by the people that own the land near the rivers and lakes. This is a very important law because water is scarce in some parts of the Southwest. This law makes it possible for water to be transported to other parts of the country so that cities can develop and people can live and grow things where water is not so plentiful.

Mexican law introduced the idea of community property, which states that when a man and woman marry, the property of one becomes the property of the other. This is an important protection for women and children.

During the Gold Rush, the only way the early miners had to settle a mining dispute was the knowledge that the Mexican miners had of mining law. Spanish-Mexican law allowed the person who discovered the ore and worked the mine to "stake a claim" on the mine. If the person did not work the mine, then he lost the mine, and it went into the hands of another. These early day Spanish laws passed into the Mexican legal system and when the United States needed mining laws, they based them on the Mexican laws.

Based on the laws which have been passed to us from Spain and Mexico, who has rights in the following cases?

1. You need some water for your crops, but the river is five miles away and runs through someone else's land. What right do you have to get water from that river?

2. A wealthy man marries a woman whose only possession is a horse. After the marriage, who owns the horse? What does the woman own?

3. You discovered gold on some land, filed a claim and began to work the mine. After a while, you can't get any more gold out of your claim, and you move on to look for another place to mine. Someone moves onto the place you left and finds more gold. Whose gold is it?

23

GA1324

¡Viva La Causa!

CESAR CHAVEZ
Union Organizer, Humanist
1927

CESAR CHAVEZ was born on a farm owned by his grandparents near Yuma, Arizona. When his grandparents purchased this land it was a barren field, and through their hard work they turned it into a thriving farm. Cesar enjoyed growing up on his grandparents' farm with his five brothers and sisters. He loved the fields and trees around his home and could often be found in his favorite tree when it was time for him to come in from outdoors. It was during the time of the Great Depression, with many people out of work, that the family lost their farm because there was no money to pay the property taxes. It was also at this time that young Cesar's life changed.

The family moved to Delano, California, and became farm workers following and harvesting the seasonal crops. When Cesar was ten life became much harder for his family, and he began to work in the fields of Delano. Often when his family was looking for work, their car became their home, and sometimes they would gather with other migrant families under a bridge for shelter. Cesar attended school when he could. Some of the schools were segregated and separated the children of the farm worker families from the other children. By the time he was in the seventh grade he had been to thirty-seven schools.

When Cesar was fifteen, he began following the crops on his own. What he experienced as a farm worker made him wonder why people had to live under such terrible conditions. He observed that farm workers and their families often went hungry when there was no work. He saw crowded, dirty labor camps, people doing backbreaking "stoop labor" for little pay and pesticides being sprayed from airplanes on fields where people worked. Cesar learned that farm workers died younger than other workers, had more sickness and accidents and their babies often died at birth. He was troubled by what he saw and wanted to change these conditions.

Cesar, who had little formal education, taught himself to read and began to read the writings of Mahatma Gandhi, a great leader in India who won freedom for his people with his nonviolent revolution against the British. Cesar also admired Martin Luther King, Jr., another great leader who organized poor people so they could gain their dignity through non-violent means. Cesar admired both men for their ability to win battles through nonviolent means. He wanted to do the same.

GA1324

In 1952 Cesar Chávez began to work with Fred Ross, a man who believed that people should organize to solve their problems. They went house to house to organize Mexican Americans and formed Community Service Organizations (CSO's) throughout California to help people obtain better jobs, improve the schools and rent or purchase their own homes. They successfully registered thousands of Mexican Americans to vote. Cesar was an effective organizer because he could speak the language of the people and because he had spent his life working in the fields. As he traveled throughout California, he realized that the only way living conditions for farm workers would improve was to organize them into a union of their own.

With his knowledge of organizing and the family's life savings of $1200, Cesar, his wife Helen and their children returned to Delano to begin a "grass roots" movement to organize farm workers into a union. They named their organization the United Farm Workers (UFW). It took many years of hard work and sacrifice before Cesar and his followers realized their dream. They encountered laws that forbade farm workers from having the same rights to organize a union as other workers, and they had to fight for better laws.

Among the achievements that Cesar is famous for in his struggle for the union are the grape strike in Delano that lasted five years, his hunger fasts to focus national attention on the farm workers' problems and the 300-mile protest march from Delano to Sacramento, the state capital of California, in 1966. The people in the march carried banners with a black eagle that read ¡HUELGA! (Strike!) and ¡Viva la causa! (Long live our cause!). The marchers wanted the state government to pass laws which would permit farm workers to organize into a union and make agreements with their bosses to obtain better wages and working conditions. They were eventually successful in getting the government to pass these laws.

Besides fighting for better wages, the union has provided leadership in setting up educational programs, credit unions and cooperative stores. These services will help farm workers improve their lives. Above all, Cesar has made people aware of the struggles of the farm workers for better pay, safer working conditions and child care needs. He has done it through nonviolent tactics and has fasted for as long as thirty days to demonstrate his concern for the farm workers. Cesar Chávez and the movement he leads recognize the dignity of the farm worker.

¡HUELGA!

¡VIVA LA CAUSA! (vee-vah   lah   cah-oo-sah)
CESAR CHAVEZ (say-sar   chah-ves)
¡HUELGA! (oo-el-gah)

25

GA1324

BOYCOTT AND STRIKE

Boycott and *strike* are two important words in labor negotiations. Look up each of the words in a dictionary and write the definitions on the lines below.

boycott _____

_____

strike _____

_____

In what ways are these two methods alike?

1. _____

2. _____

3. _____

4. _____

5. _____

In what ways are these two methods different?

1. _____

2. _____

3. _____

4. _____

5. _____

GA1324

NONVIOLENCE

Cesar believed in organizing and using nonviolent ways to change things. His heroes were Mahatma Gandhi and Martin Luther King, Jr., who also advocated that people change their conditions through protesting in a nonviolent way.

Think about something significant in this world that you would like to change. Then think of some nonviolent ways in which you could do something to change the conditions. Write about what you would try to change and how.

_____

(title)

_____
_____
_____
_____
_____
_____
_____
_____
_____
_____
_____
_____
_____
_____
_____
_____
_____
_____
_____
_____

IDEAS

Greenhouse Effect ● Discrimination ● Disappearing Animals ● Cutting Down Forests

---

GA1324

LA UNION

DOLORES FERNANDEZ HUERTA
Labor Organizer, Lobbyist, Picket Captain
1930

DOLORES FERNANDEZ HUERTA is well-known throughout the world because of the important work she does with the United Farm Workers of America, a union devoted to improving working conditions for farm workers. Having been a farm worker herself, Dolores knows firsthand what it is to work very hard for minimum wages and of the poor conditions for many farm workers. She remembers that often there were no toilets in the fields and only one cup available for an entire field of workers to drink from. The farm workers' only alternative was to quit their jobs if they were not satisfied with these conditions.

Her concern for the working conditions of farm workers and her determination to better their lives brought her to the top of the United Farm Workers Union (UFW) as vice-president. In this position she was influential in establishing the union's policy of using nonviolence to settle strikes. Dolores was often the only woman at the bargaining table, negotiating contracts and agreements with the farmers. In 1970 she helped to settle the DELANO Grape Strike, a strike that had gone on for five years.

Like many Mexican Americans, Dolores Huerta's family roots are deep and go back to the seventeenth century. She was born to a miner and a migrant agricultural worker in Dawson, New Mexico, a mining town in northeastern New Mexico. When she was still a young girl, her family left Dawson and moved to Stockton in the central valley of California, where she grew up and became a teacher.

During the 1950's, Dolores Huerta met CESAR CHAVEZ through the Community Service Organization (CSO), which he had helped to organize in Mexican American communities. When Cesar left the CSO to form the United Farm Workers of America (UFW), Dolores Huerta made the decision to leave her job as a teacher and to help him organize farm workers. She believed that she could do more for the farm worker children who came to her class hungry and without shoes by improving working conditions for their families.

Dolores Huerta spent the 1960's organizing farm workers in the central valleys of California. She also spent time in Sacramento, the state capital, trying to educate legislators about the bad working conditions of the farm workers and enlisting their support for the union cause. Dolores was very effective because she never forgot what it was like to be a farm worker.

This quiet, dedicated and unassuming woman has spent most of her life pursuing justice for farm workers that work in the fields from sunrise to sunset putting food on our tables. In her work with the union, Dolores became an effective politician and speaker on behalf of farm workers, who often have no one to speak for them. Through her efforts and that of the UFW, working conditions for the farm workers have improved.

LA UNION (lah   oo-nee-<u>on</u>)
DOLORES HUERTA (do-<u>lor</u>-es   oo-<u>err</u>-tah)
DELANO (day-<u>lah</u>-no)
CESAR CHAVEZ (<u>say</u>-sar   <u>chah</u>-ves)

28

ORGANIZING

One of the most effective ways to change conditions in this country is to create an organization of the people affected and who support la causa to make things better. Below are the names of several organizations in the Mexican American community which are dedicated to bettering conditions in society for Mexican Americans. Write the acronym for each of the organziations.

1. Mexican American Legal Defense and Education Fund   M A L D E F

2. League of United Latin American Citizens   — — — — —

3. Mexican American Political Association   — — — —

4. Association of Mexican American Educators   — — — —

5. United Farm Workers   — — —

6. National Association for Bilingual Education   — — — —

From the list of names above, write in the acronym of the organization you feel best fits the description of each organization below.

1. _____   Teachers and school personnel who promote the better education of Mexican American students and raise money for scholarships

2. _____   One of the older social organizations dedicated to many social projects, including a program for teaching basic English words

3. _____   Lawyers who take cases to defend the civil rights of Mexican Americans and raise money for scholarships

4. _____   Group interested in registering Mexican Americans to vote and in supporting candidates for political office

5. _____   A union of people who work at farm labor and want better conditions

6. _____   Teachers and educators who support teaching students skills in both Spanish and English

CAMPESINA

ISABEL E. HERNANDEZ
Migrant Farm Worker
1912

Migrant workers lead very hard lives traveling from place to place, working on farms picking fruits and vegetables for our tables. Many times these families move so often that their children attend several schools in one year, and they usually don't stay in one place long enough to make friends. Sometimes families travel together and when they do, there are friends enough for everyone. Migrant families sometimes look forward to going to particular campsites because there they will see friends they may not have seen since the last season, which could have been as long as the year before. These families must be very organized when they travel because they carry with them all their belongings.

Such a family was that of ISABEL E. HERNANDEZ. She remembers back when she was a young girl her family lived in tents which had dirt floors and a flap for a door. Wherever they traveled they carried their tents with them. Later the farmers were required to supply the farm workers with floors and screen doors. She remembers that things were better after this because the tents were more comfortable. The smaller families had one tent and the larger families had two. They would place a tarp over the tent to keep out the moisture and the rain. At night they would roll out their bedding and everyone would sleep in the same tent.

In the morning the migrant workers would take up their bedding, cook their breakfast and prepare their lunch to take to the fields. Isabel remembers that her mother would start a pot of beans at night on a coal oil stove and by morning the beans were done. Her mother got up at 4:00 a.m. every morning to start making a stack of TORTILLAS for her family to enjoy. She began by sitting on a box and placing a flat board on her lap so that she could roll the tortillas. Then she would place the tortillas on a hot COMAL to cook. The tortillas were used to make TACOS for lunch. Isabel remembers that her mother always left the fields where they all worked before the rest of the family, to start a little fire with twigs on which to heat the family's lunch.

Their breakfast consisted of hot oatmeal, toast with butter and coffee. There was always a big pot of coffee, and the family drank it with lots of milk. Their supper consisted of potatoes with canned meats, usually corned beef or sardines. They always used onions and garlic, tomato sauce and some type of beans. They used dried beans and canned foods because there was no way to keep their food from spoiling. The family never lacked food and Isabel was always surprised at what her mother could turn out on a two-burner stove.

These families, including the children, worked throughout the Southwest. Isabel remembers that they picked cotton in Firebaugh, California, for three months out of every year. In those days (1927) the cotton was hard to take out of the bolls. Later, farmers planted a different type of cotton which was easier for them to pick. The family picked cotton in winter, and the cotton had to be dry before they could pick it. When it rained they couldn't pick the cotton, so they would wait until the afternoon when the cotton was dry. That way the family made enough money for the day, and the day wasn't wasted.

Isabel remembers that she always had at least one nice dress. They dressed up on Sundays, but the rest of the week women wore men's clothing to work in. The migrant families had weekly dances, usually in old, abandoned schoolhouses. Anyone who had a guitar or a violin or any musical instrument would play and they would all dance. This is how they entertained themselves. They also celebrated people's birthdays and holidays this way. The migrants had no radios and used coal oil lamps for light. At night they made big bonfires, and if there was a good storyteller, they spent their time both telling and listening to stories. Someone always played the guitar and the people sang. Isabel remembers one man that could play and sing for many nights without ever repeating a song.

This was a long time ago, but migrant families still work and live in much the same way as they did then. They still travel together throughout the Southwest, picking fruits, vegetables and many other crops that benefit all of us. They are a proud and dignified people doing a service for all of us.

CAMPESINA (cam-pay-<u>see</u>-nah)
ISABEL HERNANDEZ (ee-sah-<u>bel</u>   ayr-<u>nahn</u>-days)
TORTILLAS (tor-<u>tee</u>-yahs)
COMAL (co-<u>mahl</u>)
TACOS (<u>tah</u>-cos)

GA1324

PICKING THE CROPS

Isabel, her family and many countless others follow the seasons of the crops from place to place, from harvest to harvest. Here is a crossword puzzle containing many of the crops that are picked in the Southwest and many of the foods that have been harvested since the time of the Spaniards and the missions.

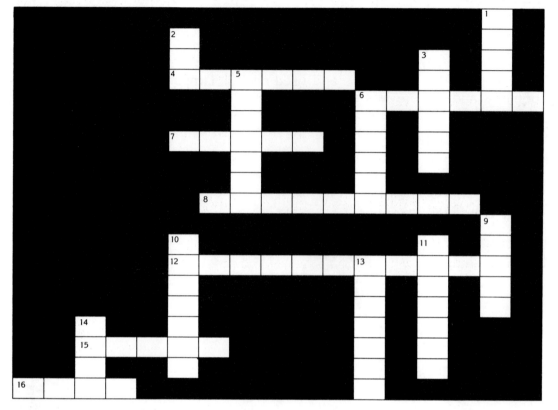

ACROSS
4. California is the leading state in growing this crop.
6. _____ can be topped on a pizza.
7. The outer skin of a _____ feels fuzzy at times.
8. This fruit makes a tasty jam.
12. The big, juicy seeds are eaten instead of the whole fruit.
15. A squeeze of a _____ will make almost anything sour.
16. This fruit is a cousin of the lemon.

DOWN
1. America is known for homemade _____ pie.
2. A _____ tree has big, green leaves.
3. Most people like _____ and sour cream on their potatoes.
5. Vegetarian sandwiches usually have _____ sprouts in them.
6. Vitamin C is found in an _____ .
9. _____ bread is high in nutritional value.
10. Looks like a peach, but smaller
11. Chocolate chip cookies can be made with _____ .
13. _____ are found quite frequently in candy bars.
14. A prune is a dried _____ .

WORD BANK
walnuts
peach
lime
alfalfa
grapes
apricot
plum
apple
raspberry
lemon
orange
fig
olives
chives
wheat
almonds
pomegranate

"DE COLORES"

When the migrants gathered around the campfires, they often sang many traditional Mexican songs. One such song is "DE COLORES," which also became identified with the farm worker movement.

DE COLORES	COLORS
De colores, de colores se visten los campos en la primavera. De colores, de colores son los pajarillos que vienen de afuera. De colores, de colores es el arco iris que vemos lucir— Y por eso los grandes amores de muchos colores me gustan a mí, Y por eso los grandes amores de muchos colores me gustan a mí.	Colors, the fields are dressed with the colors of the spring. Colors, colors of the birds that come from afar. Colors, colors of the rainbow that we see shine— That's why the loves of my life I like to imagine in many colors. That's why the loves of my life I like to imagine in many colors.
Canta el gallo canta el gallo con el qui ri qui ri qui ri qui ri quí La gallina, la gallina con su ca ra ca ra ca ra ca ra cá Los pollitos, los pollitos con el pío pío pío pío pí . . . Y por eso los grandes amores de muchos colores me gustan a mí Y por eso los grandes amores de muchos colores me gustan a mí.	The rooster sings the rooster sings his "cock-a-doodle-do" The hen, the hen sings "cluck, cluck, cluck, cluck" The chicks, the chicks sing "peep, peep, peep, peep". . . That's why the loves of my life I like to imagine in many colors. That's why the loves of my life I like to imagine in many colors.

By comparing the Spanish and English versions of this song, figure out what each of the following Spanish words means:

1. campos _____
2. primavera _____
3. arco iris _____

4. gallo _____
5. gallina _____
6. pollitos _____

In Spanish the animals make different sounds. What, according to the song, are the sounds made by these animals?

7. rooster _____
8. hen _____
9. chicken _____

Practice making these sounds in Spanish.

DE COLORES (day   co-lor-ays)

GA1324

LOS CAMPOS
(the fields)

The song "De Colores" is about colors of the fields and camps where the farm workers lived. They suggest a landscape. Draw or paint the scene suggested in the song.

LOS CAMPOS (lohs cahm-pohs)

GA1324

TEATRO

LUIS VALDEZ
Playwright, Poet, Actor, Director
1940

As long as there have been Mexican American people in the Southwest, there has been teatro. As early as 1598, plays depicting explorations into New Mexico were staged by the men of the Spanish exploration of JUAN DE OÑATE. In the 1800's, theater troupes from Mexico performed musicals and melodramas throughout California. Many plays in Spanish and English have been performed since then. More recently, popular plays written by Mexican Americans have depicted the lives of Mexicans in the Southwest. The plays have also helped to unify Mexican Americans and show their resistance to the injustices they have undergone. These acting companies performed in theaters and in tents for migrant farm workers.

One person who has followed these traditions of theater is LUIS VALDEZ. Luis Valdez has become known for his plays and his theater group, EL TEATRO CAMPESINO, but his beginnings were humble. Born in Delano, California, to migrant farm worker parents, he began working in the fields at the age of six and spent his youth moving with his family as they followed the crops. As a young boy, Luis entertained his family with puppet shows. When he was older, he received a scholarship to attend college in San Jose, California, and graduated in 1964. Luis liked to write poetry and plays. The Drama Department of San Jose State College produced his first play called "The Shrunken Head of Pancho Villa."

Luis Valdez became involved with the farm workers and their strike for better working conditions during the Delano Grape Strike in 1965. He began his theater group by using farm workers as actors and having them re-create what happened on the picket line that day. The group performed in the fields, often on flatbed trucks, and used these short plays to dramatize the problems of the farm workers. This theater brought attention to the grape strike and the boycott and helped people sympathize with the farm workers and gain support for the HUELGA (strike).

Luis Valdez called these improvisations ACTOS. He had experience in theater and had performed in plays, but the farm workers had no professional acting experience. Luis gave them lessons and direction. Because the plays were performed outdoors in open spaces, it was not always possible to use elaborate stage props or costumes. Instead, Luis often used masks and signs around the actors' necks to identify the characters. A favorite was a pig face mask to depict a bad boss.

LUIS VALDEZ (loo-ees   val-des)
JUAN DE OÑATE (oo-ahn   day   oohn-yah-tay)
EL TEATRO CAMPESINO (el   tay-ah-tro   cam-pay-see-no)
HUELGA (oo-el-gah)
ACTOS (ahc-tos)

After two years Luis Valdez and his teatro left the farm worker union and the strike to devote more time to developing their theater group. El Teatro Campesino has toured several times in Europe, as well as in the United States, and has received national recognition and won many awards. In 1967 they were invited to perform before a Senate Subcommittee on Agricultural Labor in Washington, D.C. That year they moved to Delano, California, then later to Fresno and finally to San Juan Bautista where they established El Teatro Campesino in an old packing shed.

Luis continues to educate and entertain his audiences as he moves into television and film productions, first with the movie version of his own play *Zoot Suit* and then with a major motion picture he wrote based on the life of Richie Valens, *La Bamba.* Still he expresses the issues that confront Chicanos, just as the early day actors did before him.

DISCUSS

Reread the portrait of Luis and find the following words which describe a people:

Mexican	Mexican American
Spanish	Spanish-speaking
Chicano	Hispanic

How do these words differ from each other? In what ways are they similar?

Which word do you think Luis would use to describe himself?

PLAYS

Below are the names of some of Luis Valdez's original plays and some created by his company El Teatro Campesino. Write in the name of the play that seems to fit the description best. Look for clues in the dates and the Spanish words that look like English words.

> *I Don't Have to Show You No Stinking Badges!*   *Zoot Suit*
>
> *¡Bandido!*   *EL Fin del Mundo*   *La Bamba*
>
>   *Soldado Razo*   *Corridos*

1. _____ A movie about the life of Richie Valens, a young Mexican American singer and composer who became a music star in the 1950's, but then lost his life in a plane crash. The title refers to the song he made popular.

2. _____ A play about the life and legend of Tiburcio Vasquez, a notorious bandit in California during the years 1873 to 1875.

3. _____ A story about life and death, with death played in a skeleton costume. The title means "the end of the world."

4. _____ A selection of popular Mexican songs, each one telling a story. The title refers to the name in Spanish for this kind of song.

5. _____ A play about Los Angeles in the 1940's and a young Mexican American accused of a murder. It became the first play by a Chicano playwright to be produced on Broadway in New York, and later it was made into a movie. The title refers to the clothes many young Mexican American men liked to wear in those days.

6. _____ An antiwar play about the effect of the Vietnam War on the family of a Chicano soldier who is killed.

7. _____ A play about two Chicano actors trying to become successful in Hollywood but encountering many stereotypes about Mexicans.

BANDIDO (ban-dee-do)
EL FIN DEL MUNDO (el feen del moon-do)
LA BAMBA (lah bam-bah)
SOLDADO RAZO (sol-dah-do rah-so)
CORRIDOS (cor-ree-dos)

ACTOS

Luis and his actors often used signs hung around their necks and masks to show the parts they were playing. The most popular masks were the pig, which represented the boss, and the skull, which represented death.

The plays were created through improvisation, making up the story and dialogue as you go along. First there is the theme for the play; then characters are named and the actors assume the part.

How would it feel to be an actor in this kind of troupe? What type of character would you like to play?

_____

In groups, choose a theme which deals with an injustice—someone or some people being unfairly treated. Name some characters and take their parts. Then improvise—make up your play—and you have an acto.

Here are some examples for themes for your acto.

> A rule at school that you would like to change
> Allowances for kids
> Prejudices
> Copying movies and computer programs

What are some themes your group suggests?

_____

_____

_____

_____

PATRONCITO

Consider making signs and masks for the characters to wear.

Perform your acto for the rest of the class and talk with the audience afterwards about how they felt about the play.

GA1324

TEATROS

Luis Valdez's El Teatro Campesino inspired the formation of many other theater groups in the Southwest. Most of the groups use the word *teatro* in their titles, and then something to reflect that their plays come from the hearts of the people.

Here are the names of a few Chicano theater groups. Use the dictionary at the bottom to translate their names. Remember *teatro* means "theater."

1. El Teatro Campesinos _____

2. El Teatro de las Cucarachas _____

3. El Teatro del Barrio _____

4. El Teatro de la Esperanza _____

5. El Teatro del Espiritu _____

6. El Teatro de la Tierra _____

7. El Teatro de los Pobres _____

8. El Teatro de la Gente _____

9. Teatro Nuestro _____

10. El Teatro del Piojo _____

11. Teatro Jalapeño _____

DICCIONARO

DE	(day)	of
EL, LA	(el, lah)	the
LOS, LAS	(loos, lahs)	the
BARRIO	(bar-ree-o)	neighborhood
CAMPESINOS	(cam-pay-see-nos)	farm workers
CUCARACHAS	(coo-ca-rah-chahs)	cockroaches
ESPERANZA	(es-pay-rahn-sah)	hope
ESPIRITU	(es-pee-ree-too)	spirit
GENTE	(hen-tay)	people
JALAPEÑO	(hal-lah-pay-nyo)	chili pepper
PIOJO	(pee-o-ho)	flea
POBRES	(po-brays)	the poor
NUESTRO	(noo-es-tro)	our
TIERRA	(tee-ayr-ah)	earth

GA1324

ACTOR

EDWARD JAMES OLMOS
Actor, Role Model
1947

Edward James Olmos has done a lot to change people's ideas about Mexican Americans by breaking away from stereotypes. Through his choice of parts and through his portrayal of Latino characters, this actor who grew up in Boyle Heights, a Los Angeles BARRIO, has brought positive attention to the Mexican American and Latino communities.

One of the roles he made famous was that of Lieutenant MARTIN CASTILLO in *Miami Vice*. He also played EL PACHUCO in *Zoot Suit*, a play by Luis Valdez, and starred in the movie version. The play brought Eddie Olmos a Tony nomination and the Los Angeles Drama Critics Award.

In the movie *Stand and Deliver*, Eddie Olmos played the part of Jaime Escalante, the famous teacher at Garfield High School in Los Angeles, who coached his math class to winning scores on the advanced math test. This movie, which depicts students from the barrio as bright and capable of doing outstanding schoolwork, is an example of the kind of role Eddie Olmos thinks is important.

Eddie Olmos tries to be authentic in his acting. He is a very hardworking actor. For his part as Jaime Escalante, Eddie gained forty pounds and studied Escalante's voice on tapes so that he could look and sound like the famous teacher. He was nominated for an Academy Award for his role in *Stand and Deliver*.

This actor has not let all the publicity and his celebrity status get in the way of continuing to be a role model for young Mexican Americans. Edward Olmos, who grew up in a barrio, speaks to young high school audiences, stressing the importance of an education and the contribution that each can make to improve society. Eddie Olmos also visits hospitals, jails and Indian reservations with his message of hope and justice.

ACTOR (ack-<u>tohr</u>)
BARRIO (<u>bah</u>-ree-oh)
MARTIN CASTILLO (mahr-<u>teen</u>   cahs-<u>tee</u>-yo)
EL PACHUCO (el   pah-<u>choo</u>-coh)

GA1324

STAND AND DELIVER

In groups of five, make up a short play which shows a teacher as a positive role model. Have four students take the parts of students and one be the teacher. Create a scene where the teacher can do something very positive to make the students feel better about being in school and learning or a scene which makes them want to learn more.

For each group, have the "teacher" teach a different subject—math, reading, science, music, art or history.

Perform your play for the class.

ACTORS—PARTS

_____

_____

_____

_____

ASSIGNMENTS

_____

_____

_____

_____

SUMMARIZE THE PLAY.

_____

_____

_____

_____

_____

_____

_____

_____

_____

_____

_____

_____

_____

_____

_____

_____

_____

GA1324

STEREOTYPES

What is a stereotype? Look up the definition and write it below.

_____

How do people learn stereotypes about other people?

_____

_____

What are some stereotypes people might have about Mexican Americans?

_____

_____

Look at the drawings on this page. What clues do they give you about Mexican American stereotypes?

_____

_____

_____

Do you think they are accurate? Do any of the portraits in this book fit the image of the stereotypes?

_____

_____

_____

What are role models? Why are they important to a group of people?

_____

_____

_____

_____

_____

_____

GA1324

JUAN ALONZO (ah-lohn-so) was born in Texas and grew up both in Mexico and Texas. He became interested in the arts, theater and making films. Some of the films he worked on were *Chinatown, Harold and Maude, Sounder* and the *Bad News Bears*.

LYNDA CORDOBA CARTER was born in Arizona of a Mexican mother and an English father. At the age of fifteen she began acting and went on to be featured in the television series *Wonder Woman* in 1976. She was Miss U.S.A. in the Miss World contest in the 1970's. Linda is a beautiful woman who owns her own production company.

RICARDO MONTALBAN (mohn-tahl-bahn) was born in Mexico and moved to Los Angeles at the age of sixteen. After learning acting in New York and making his first films in Mexico, Ricardo returned again in 1945 to the U.S. and took many parts in films, some of them as stereotyped Latins or Indians. Later he gained success in television, particularly as the star of *Fantasy Island*. He was concerned for Hispanic actors and started a group called Nosotros (We) in 1969.

ANTHONY (RUDOLFO OAXACA) QUINN was born in northern Mexico in the middle of the Mexican Revolution in 1916. His mother was Mexican, his father Irish. When the family came to the U.S., he had to drop out of school to help support the family and took all kinds of jobs, including parts in the movies as an Indian, a villain and a Latin. By the 1980's he had appeared in over two hundred films, including *Viva Zapata, Guns of Navarone, Lawrence of Arabia, Shoes of the Fisherman* and *Zorba the Greek*. He also toured in the play of *Zorba*. Anthony Quinn is also a painter, writer and sculptor.

GILBERT ROLAND was born in Mexico and came first to Texas, then California, where he got small parts in movies in the 1920's. He became a star in Hollywood at a time when the movies were silent. His real name was Luis Antonio Alonso, but he changed it to Gilbert Roland by combining the names of his two favorite actors, John Gilbert and Ruth Roland. He appeared in over sixty films.

CARMEN ZAPATA (sah-pah-tah) was born in New York. Her parents were from Mexico and Argentina. She studied acting and played on Broadway. In Hollywood she first found parts only in stereotyped roles. She had better luck in television. For a while she was Doña Luz in the children's bilingual show *Villa Alegre* (Happy Village). In 1973 she began her own theater company in Los Angeles. It is called the Bilingual Foundation of the Arts, and it presents plays where one night they are in Spanish, the next in English.

GA1324

CANCIONES

LINDA RONSTADT
Singer
1947

One of the most important Mexican American traditions in music is that of musical families. These musical families keep their style of music alive by making it a part of their family life, often singing and playing together at family gatherings and also in the evenings after the day's work is done. Entire families will sing and play musical instruments, and this becomes an important way for music to be passed from one generation to the next. The children of these families who have grown up with the music often become fine musicians themselves.

Linda Ronstadt was born into one of these well-known musical families in Tucson, Arizona, just sixty miles from the Mexican border. Part of Linda's childhood memories are of listening to Mexican music at family gatherings. Her father, Gilbert Ronstadt, was a musician who appeared on local radio stations. He introduced Linda and her brother and sister to Mexican music. Gilbert Ronstadt became the biggest musical influence on Linda's life.

Linda became a famous singer with many platinum and gold albums to her credit. She was even invited to sing at President Carter's inauguration. As her career developed, she tried many different styles of music, from rock and roll to country music. She even starred in Broadway plays and appeared in movies. Linda Ronstadt is known as a person who takes many risks with her music because she is always willing to try something new.

One of the biggest musical risks of her career was when she decided to make an album in Spanish. Some people thought perhaps no one would buy it. But Linda had always wanted to make an album of familiar Spanish songs that she had heard her father sing. The album, which was called *CANCIONES DE MI PADRE* (Songs of My Father), became very popular and stimulated interest in MARIACHI and RANCHERA music among the general public.

Linda Ronstadt, who is very proud of her heritage, enjoyed making the album in Spanish and considers it a tribute to her father and to her background. On the jacket cover of the album *Canciones de Mi Padre*, Linda says:

> Many of the songs on this record were passed on through my father to me, and others I have learned through my continuing interest in the great vocal traditions of Mexico. These songs comprise a tradition both of my family and of a country which has made profound contributions to the world of music. They are a living memory of heartfelt experience.
>
> L. Ronstadt, 1987
> Elektra/Asylum Records

CANCIONES DE MI PADRE (cahn-see <u>ohn</u>-ays   day   mee   <u>pah</u>-dray)
MARIACHI (mah-ree-<u>ah</u>-chee)
RANCHERA (rahn-<u>che</u>-rah)

GA1324

CANCIONES

The songs on Linda's album are all traditional Mexican songs. Below are the titles in Spanish of the songs on the album. Try to match the titles with the English translations below. Use a Spanish-English dictionary if you need help.

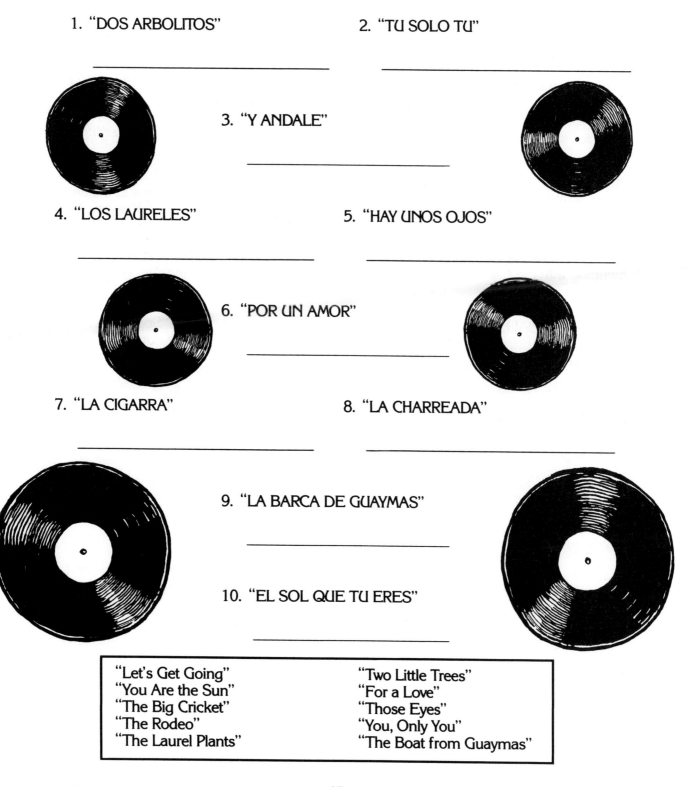

1. "DOS ARBOLITOS"

2. "TU SOLO TU"

3. "Y ANDALE"

4. "LOS LAURELES"

5. "HAY UNOS OJOS"

6. "POR UN AMOR"

7. "LA CIGARRA"

8. "LA CHARREADA"

9. "LA BARCA DE GUAYMAS"

10. "EL SOL QUE TU ERES"

"Let's Get Going"
"You Are the Sun"
"The Big Cricket"
"The Rodeo"
"The Laurel Plants"

"Two Little Trees"
"For a Love"
"Those Eyes"
"You, Only You"
"The Boat from Guaymas"

45

GA1324

THE MUSIC OF MEXICAN AMERICANS

Mexican American people are talented music makers, and music is very much a part of their lives. There have been many influences on Mexican music, and these influences have produced different musical styles. Music is one way different cultures come together to influence each other and blend to create new and different sounds.

Mexican music, and later the music of the Southwest, had its roots in early Indian, Spanish, African, Caribbean, German and Czechoslovakian music, to name just some styles that influenced it. During the Spanish colonial period, when the Spaniards were trying to change the Indian ways of life, the one tradition that was left to the native peoples of "New Spain" was that of their music.

Music was the one trait that was compatible with the Spanish ideas and accepted by them. The Spaniards often used music as a way of converting the Indians to Christian beliefs and encouraged the native peoples to use their own music as a form of worship. Musicians were so respected by the Spanish colonizers that they were exempt from paying taxes.

African and Afro-Caribbean music influenced areas settled by Africans, as in the state of Vera Cruz in Mexico. The famous marimba seems to have been first introduced by these early people. Later, with the arrival of Central Europeans such as the Germans and Czechs, with their accordions and polkas, a newer influence (called Tex Mex music) was introduced.

The music of Mexican Americans is as varied as the people themselves and is continually blending with the older traditions of the music to form newer styles.

MEXICAN BALLADS, or CORRIDOS, are popular throughout the Southwest. They are usually songs that tell about the lives of heroes, or just about the common people. Many of them are songs of love.

MARIACHI MUSIC uses brass and string instruments and is among the most well-known "Mexican music" and very popular. Mariachi musicians can be heard at fiestas or many other public occasions in the Southwest as well as in Mexico. Each year in Tucson, Arizona, there is a festival of mariachis, lasting several days and featuring the best of the mariachis in the Southwest.

TEX MEX MUSIC is strictly music of the Southwest and was introduced by Germans in Texas around the early 1900's. The music uses a lot of accordion and polkas.

GA1324

MUSICIANS

JOAN BAEZ (ba-<u>yes</u>) was born in New York. Her father was born in Mexico. She grew up loving music and also became interested in the social issues of her time. She made her debut in 1959 as a folksinger and soon became known nationwide. In the 1960's and the 1970's she participated in antiwar rallies and demonstrations for equal rights and for the farm workers. She marched with Martin Luther King, Jr., and with Cesar Chávez. She toured in Europe and Latin America and has made over thirty albums. One of her best known songs is "The Night They Drove Old Dixie Down."

VIKKI CARR was born in Texas and grew up in California. Her real name is Florencia Bicentia de Casillas Martínez Cardona. She started out singing in a band and became a top vocalist in the early 1960's. She toured internationally and performed at the White House and for the Queen of England. She also became a leading singer in Mexico, singing in Spanish. She has established scholarships for Mexican American students and donated her services to community events.

PETE ESCOVEDO (es-co-<u>vay</u>-do) was born in California and grew up with Latin music because his father sang in Mexican bands. Pete played drums in the 1960's with the Carlos Santana band and then formed the group Azteca with his brother Coke. He now performs alone and sometimes with his daughter, Sheila E.

PEDRO GONZALES, JR., (gohn-<u>zal</u>-es) was born in 1895 in Mexico and came with his family to Los Angeles in 1920. He formed a musical group called Los Madrugadores and had a radio program early in the morning. He began speaking out against injustices against Mexican Americans and was arrested in 1933 on false charges. He spent six years in prison before he was released, and then he was deported to Mexico. In 1971 he was allowed to return. His story is told in a movie called *Break of Dawn*.

GA1324

EDUARDO (LALO) GUERRERO (gayr-ray-ro) was born to a poor family in Arizona and developed a talent for piano and guitar, singing songs his mother taught him. He played in a small band in New York and moved to California after the war, where he became successful in night clubs. He has written over two hundred songs and recorded more than ten albums, singing ballads and corridos, and sometimes comical songs. He is also the voice in Spanish of La Ardillitas, the Chipmunks.

TRINIDAD LOPEZ (lo-pes) was born in Texas and grew up to play in a band which went to Los Angeles, where he found work as a solo musician. In 1963 he had a hit album, selling over a million copies. His number one song "If I Had a Hammer" became a hit in twenty-three countries. He made over fourteen albums and appeared in movies and television. Much of his music is called Latin Rock.

RAFAEL MENDEZ (men-des) was born in Mexico in 1906 to a musical family. He even played the trumpet in bullrings before coming to the U.S. in 1926. Here he played in the Russ Morgan Band and later in the Metro Goldyn Mayer Studio Orchestra. He played on over one hundred and fifty albums, and in 1964 he was the first trumpeter to play a solo performance at Carnegie Hall. He died in 1981.

LYDIA MENDOZA (men-do-sa) was born in 1916 in Texas and grew up on the border. Her family was musical, and she learned guitar and violin early. She toured the Southwest, playing with her family. Later she was discovered and offered a recording contract. She recorded thirty-five albums and made many folk festival appearances in the Southwest.

RICHIE VALENS grew up in the 1950's in California. His real name was Ricardo Valenzuela (vah-len-sway-lah), but he changed his name and became a young recording hit with his original song "Donna." His recording of the traditional Mexican song "La Bamba" was upbeat and popular for rock and roll taste. Unfortunately, his career was cut short when he died at an early age in a plane crash. His story is told in the movie *La Bamba*.

GA1324

MUSIC

Mexican Americans have excelled in many varied types of music. From the list of famous singers, find recordings and listen to their music. Then fill in the name of the singer that best fits the style of music described.

Love Songs   _____

Latin Rock and Roll   _____

Folk Songs and Ballads   _____

Latin Jazz   _____

Mexican Trio Music   _____

Big Band Orchestras   _____

Texas Mexican Music   _____

Rock and Roll   _____

Ballads and Corridos   _____

Can you find examples of Mexican music or music that is a combination of styles, including Mexican influences? What instruments do you hear in the music? Where or with whom is this particular type of music popular?

GA1324

NAMES

You may have noticed some things about names of Mexican Americans, some of the features which are in the Spanish language.

First of all, in Spanish and traditional Mexican names, everyone has two last names instead of one.

FLORENCIA MARTINEZ CARDONA

FLORENCIA is the first name. MARTINEZ is the last name (of her father), and CARDONA is the second last name (her mother's maiden name).

If you were to follow this system of using two last names, what would be your name? _____

_____

Other names in your family: _____

_____

_____

When two people marry, the husband's name stays the same, but the woman adds her husband's first last name. For example, if FLORENCIA MARTINEZ CARDONA married JORGE SANCHEZ ALONSO, her name would be:

FLORENCIA MARTINEZ CARDONA DE SANCHEZ

Most Mexican Americans, however, do not follow the traditional ways and use only one last name, the father's, although recently many Mexican American women have begun using their maiden names and their husbands' last names together, like:

FLORENCIA MARTINEZ SANCHEZ

Singers, actresses and actors often change their names completely and take "stage" names, or sometimes they have used English versions of their names. Find the real names of the following stars:

1. Florencia Martínez Cardona _____

2. Luis Antonio Alonso _____

3. Antonio (Rudolfo Oaxaca) Quinn _____   _____

4. Ricardo Valenzuela _____

5. Sheila Escovedo _____

GA1324

CHOOSE A NAME

Here are some first names in Spanish and some of the nicknames people use. Can you find the equivalent of your name and those of your friends? Would you prefer to choose a new Spanish name?

100 Nombres Masculinos

Abrahán	Domingo	Ignacio/Nacho	Mauricio
Adalberto/Beto	Edmundo	Jaime	Miguel/Miguelito
Adolfo	Eduardo	Javier	Nicolás/Nico
Alberto/Beto	Eliseo	Jerónimo/Jero	Octavio
Alejandro	Emilio	Jesús	Pablo/Pablito
Alfonso/Poncho	Enrique/Quique	Joaquín	Pedro/Pedrito
Alfredo	Ernesto	Jorge	Rafael
Alonso	Esteban	José/Pepe	Ramón/Ramoncito
Andrés	Ezequiel	José/Pepito	Raúl
Angel	Federico	José/Joselito	Reginaldo
Antonio/Toño	Felipe	Juan/Juanito	Reymundo
Arturo	Félix	Julián	Reynaldo
Agustín	Efrén	Julio	Ricardo
Benito	Fernando/Fernán	Lázaro	Rigoberto/Beto
Benjamín	Francisco/Paco	Leonardo	Roberto/Beto
Bernardo	Gabriel	Lorenzo	Rogelio
Bruno	Gerónimo/Gero	Lucío	Rolando
Carlos/Carlitos	Gilberto/Beto	Luis	Rosario/Chayo
Cecilio	Gonzalo	Manolo	Salvador/Chava
Dagoberto/Beto	Gregorio/Goyo	Manuel/Manuelito	Samuel
Daniel	Guillermo/Memo	Marcos	Sebastián
David	Guadalupe/Lupe	Mario	Simón
Demetrio	Herminio	Martín/Martincito	Tomás
Diego	Hilario	Mateo	Valentín
Dionisio	Horacio	Matiás	Vicente

100 Nombres Femeninos

Adela/Adelita	Clara	Guillermina	Natividad
Aída	Consuelo/Chelo	Herlinda	Noemí
Alicia/Licha	Concepción	Hortensia	Norma
Amalia	Cristina	Inés	Ofelia
Amparo	Delia	Isabel/Chavela	Olivia
Ana/Anita	Dolores/Lola	Josefa	Patricia
Angélica	Dorotea	Josefina	Paula/Paulina
Andrea	Elena/Nena	Juana/Juanita	Paz
Antonia/Toña	Elisa	Julia/Julieta	Pilar
Armida	Elvia	Laura/Laurita	Raquel/Raquelita
Aurelia	Emilia	Leonora	Rebeca
Aurora	Enriqueta/Quica	Leticia	Rita
Bárbara	Esperanza	Lidia	Rosa/Rosita
Beatriz	Estela	Lucía/Luz	Rosalía/Chayo
Belita	Ester	Luisa	Rosaura
Berta	Eugenia	Linda	Sara
Blanca	Eulalia	Manuela	Silvia
Caridad	Eva	Marcia	Sofía
Carlota	Felipa/Lipa	Margarita	Soledad
Carmela	Felisa	María	Suzana
Carmen	Florentina/Tina	Mariana	Teresa/Tere
Carolina	Francisca	Maricela	Trinidad
Catalina	Gloria	Marta	Virginia
Cecilia	Graciela	Martina	Ynés
Celia	Guadalupe/Lupe	Mónica	Yolanda

GA1324

MURALES

MURALS

Murals are one of the most popular art forms and continue a tradition of art that is very Mexican. Murals usually depict a scene or story, or even a history of people. Although one person may design the mural, several artists usually work on it together.

Make a class mural, depicting a scene. One idea to consider is the history of the town in which you live. Make drawings of the early days of the town when it was settled, some of the outstanding landmarks of the town and history and a scene of the present day problems.

Murals often give messages to the viewer. They often make political statements. What message about your town can you include as part of the art?

Sketch your mural here.

MURALES (moo-rah-les)

ARTISTS

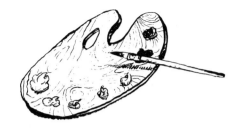

MANUEL GREGORIO ACOSTA (ah-cos-tah) was born in 1921 in Mexico but studied art in Texas and California. In the 1950's he painted murals in Texas and New Mexico and had several art exhibitions. He painted the 1969 portrait of Cesar Chávez for the cover of *Time* magazine.

ALFREDO ARREGUIN (ahr-ray-geen) was born in Mexico in 1935. He studied art and architecture in Mexico, and later in Seattle, Washington. He is well-known for his patterned art, large paintings of tropical scenes using many bright colors and small squares of color.

GUSTAVO ARRIOLA (ahr-ree-oh-lah) was born in 1917 in Arizona and moved to Los Angeles. He became a cartoonist and developed a comic strip "Gordo," which began in 1946. In the early days, Gordo was a stereotyped Mexican character. Later in the 1950's Gordo's character became less stereotyped as Gustavo himself became interested in Mexican folk art and reflected Gordo as a tour bus driver. The comic strip won several awards.

PATROCINIO BARELA (bah-ray-lah) was born in 1902 and grew up in labor camps in the Southwest, settling in New Mexico in 1930. He discovered his very extraordinary talent carving religious figures in wood and became recognized for his carvings, called "bultos." He also carved wooden doors and Spanish colonial style furniture. His carvings became collectors' items in the United States. In 1964 he died in a fire that broke out in his workshop.

JOSE ANTONIO BURCIAGA (boor-cee-ah-gah) was born in Texas in 1940 and developed a talent for both writing and art. After serving time in the Air Force, he moved to San Francisco and worked as an artist, muralist, poet and writer. Some of his writings and illustrations are humorous with a feeling of folk art.

RUPERT GARCIA (gahr-cee-ah) was born in 1941 and grew up in northern California. He developed an interest in art through his grandmother, who showed him Mexican folk art. He started an art career but then joined the Air Force. When he returned, he continued his study of art and specialized in printmaking. He used his talents to produce posters for political movements in the 1970's.

GA1324

JOSE MONTOYA (mohn-toh-ya) was born in 1932 in rural New Mexico to a migrant family, and he ended up in California. After he served in the Navy he began studying art and became part of a collective of Chicano artists in the Sacramento area, who became known as the R.C.A.F., the Royal Chicano Air Force. Their original name was the Rebel Chicano Art Front, but the initials were so much like the famous Royal Canadian Air Force, that the new title stuck and they "flew with it." José is also a poet and teacher at a college in Sacramento.

MALAQUIAS MONTOYA (mohn-toh-ya) was born in 1938 in New Mexico. In the late 1960's he studied art in California and became involved in the Chicano movement, painting posters and designs for several causes. He also participated in painting murals and in 1986 painted one in Baja, California.

MANUEL NERI (nay-ree) was born in 1930 in California and first studied engineering. After spending time in the service, in the 1950's he traveled in Mexico and studied art there and then returned to the United States. His interest is in sculpting, ceramics, bronze and marble, and he worked on many life-size human figures.

ERNESTO PALOMINO (pah-loh-mee-no) was born in 1933 in California. After spending time in the Marine Corps, he also studied art and became one of the Chicano artists of the 1960's. In some of his work he collaborated with Luis Valdez and used Chicano themes for murals. He teaches art in a college.

AMANDO PEÑA, JR., (payn-yah) was born in Texas in 1943. He became involved in Chicano causes in the 1960's and then followed a career in teaching. His watercolor paintings have themes in the styles and colors of the Southwest.

PETER RODRIGUEZ (rohd-ree-ges) was born in 1926 in California. His father was a miner, and Peter became interested in art early, especially abstract art. He traveled and exhibited several times in Mexico and became a collector of Mexican art. He also studied museum management and began first the Galeria de la Raza in 1970 in San Francisco and the Mexican Museum in 1973, also in San Francisco.

PROFIRIO SALINAS (sah-lee-nahs) was born in Texas in 1912 and showed artistic ability in his early years. He was self-taught and worked on landscape scenes, especially the landscapes of Texas. He was President Lyndon Johnson's favorite painter and had five of his paintings in the White House. Salinas died in 1973.

MANUEL UNZUETA (oon-sway-tah) was born in 1949 in Mexico but grew up in Texas and California. He became interested in art and music and the social issues of the 1960's and 1970's. He was especially interested in the muralists of Mexico and painted more than twenty murals in the Southwest. He is considered one of the top muralists in America.

GA1324

WHO PAINTED THE PICTURE?

In the frames below, the names of the artists are all mixed up. Find out who the artists are by rearranging the letters to spell the names.

1. E M O O J A T S Y O N

_____

2. N M L E N A Z U U A U E T

_____

3. N R I M A L U E N E

_____

4. S A N Q M A L I U A A Y I O O M

_____

5. E R N A F E O R D I R L U G A

_____

6. P A G A I U T R R E R C

_____

WORD BANK

José Montoya	Alfredo Arreguín
Rupert García	Manuel Unzueta
Manuel Neri	Malaquías Montoya

GA1324

EL CLAMOR PUBLICO

FRANCISCO P. RAMIREZ
Young Newspaper Publisher
1830-1890

Newspapers are an important way for people to receive information and keep themselves informed about what is happening in their communities and in the world. From the early history of the Southwest, when Spanish was the language spoken by most of the people, printing presses were used to publish newspapers. In this way the Spanish-speaking population received the information they needed in the language they understood and others could reach this audience through ads directed to them in Spanish. Even in small towns, where people could least afford to buy a newspaper, there was always someone who started a Spanish language newspaper. Oftentimes the editors of these newspapers were very brave and spoke out about the injustice they saw around them.

One such person was FRANCISCO P. RAMIREZ, who was born in Mexican California and grew up during the United States takeover of California and the Gold Rush. When he established his newspaper *El Clamor Publico* (The Public Outcry) in Los Angeles in 1855, Francisco Ramírez became the voice of the Spanish-speaking people of California and a champion of their cause. The newspaper, which he edited and published weekly from 1855 to 1859, spoke out against the widespread discrimination toward the Spanish-speaking in southern California.

Among the things Francisco spoke out against in his newspaper were the unequal treatment Mexican Americans received before the law, including being driven from the mines, problems with the courts in trying to keep their lands and the lynchings of Mexicans, which were commonplace. In 1854 there was one murder for every day in Los Angeles, with the majority of the victims being either Mexican or Indian. He called for publication of all laws in booklets and newspapers in Spanish, which had been guaranteed under the Treaty of GUADALUPE HIDALGO and the Constitution of California. He also called for the education of all children, including girls—which was a radical idea at the time—and for freedom of religion. He championed the civil rights of Mexicans and African American peoples. He wanted Mexican Americans to vote and elect people to office to stop the injustices against them. Francisco Ramírez also wanted all the people to work together because he believed it would make California strong.

El Clamor Publico was a successful newspaper and was read by everyone who wanted to know what the Mexican Americans were thinking and doing. The newspaper competed very well in sales with the other two English language newspapers that were being published in Los Angeles. Even those who did not agree with Francisco's point of view used the paper to reach the Spanish-speaking through ads. Francisco Ramírez, who was only twenty-one years old when he started the newspaper, showed what a young person with great determination and a belief in fairness and equality can accomplish.

EL CLAMOR PUBLICO (el clah-<u>mor</u>   poo-blee-co)
FRANCISCO RAMIREZ (frahn-<u>sees</u>-co   rah-<u>mee</u>-res)
GUADALUPE HIDALGO (goo-ah-dah-<u>loo</u>-pay   ee-<u>dahl</u>-go)

GA1324

INJUSTICES

Discuss in groups of four to five and assign someone to take notes on the following questions:

Francisco Ramírez wrote about injustices against the Mexican Americans in his time. What are some of those injustices?

_____

_____

_____

_____

_____

Why do you think these injustices occurred? How were people able to get away with unjust practices?

_____

_____

_____

What other groups of people have experienced injustices like the ones described by Ramírez? What was a possible underlying cause of these injustices?

_____

_____

_____

Use your group notes for a whole group discussion.

 GA1324

EDITORIALS

When a newspaper reporter or a citizen is given the opportunity to write about his opinions, it is called an editorial. Editorials are written to call attention to an injustice or to influence public opinion.

In groups of four or five, collect samples of editorials from your local newspaper. Read and discuss them. What are the writers of these editorials attempting to do?

SOME THINGS TO THINK ABOUT:

What is freedom of the press?

What rights do you have to say anything you want?

What responsibilities do you have?

Do you think everything printed in a newspaper is true?

Write an editorial on an issue about which you are concerned.

_____

(title)

_____
_____
_____
_____
_____
_____
_____
_____
_____
_____
_____
_____
_____
_____
_____

by_____

GA1324

GROUPS FOR ACTION

Even in the best of schools, there are always some things we want to make better. In groups of four to five students, develop a project of something which you consider a problem at your school. Here are some steps to take in the groups.

1. Interview other students to find out what school conditions or rules they think are unfair or want to see changed.

2. Make a list of these opinions and discuss them in your class group. Decide which problem you wish to pursue.

3. How long has this problem or condition existed?

4. What problems has this condition caused?

5. How many people has it affected?

6. What are some possible changes or solutions to make the condition better?

7. Of these solutions, which seems best?

8. If this solution were implemented, what would be the results or consequences?

9. What are some of the steps you could take to arrive at this solution?

10. Share the results with the rest of the class.

GA1324

CHICANO

RUBEN SALAZAR
Newspaper Reporter
1928-1970

RUBEN SALAZAR is an example of a courageous Mexican American newspaper and television reporter who won many awards from major newspapers in the United States for his investigative reporting. He became a voice for Mexican Americans when, toward the end of the 1960's, he was assigned by his newspaper, *The Los Angeles Times*, to write a column explaining Chicano life in Los Angeles. Rubén wrote honest essays that exposed the discrimination and prejudice Mexican Americans faced.

The articles he wrote caused controversy and brought Rubén into conflict with many important people who did not agree with what he was writing. As a result, pressure to change his stories was placed on the news media, but Rubén had the courage to continue telling the truth in his articles.

In August 1970, Rubén Salazar was assigned to cover the Chicano Moratorium, a national rally held in Los Angeles which attracted Mexican Americans from all over the United States to protest the Vietnam War. During the Moratorium, riots broke out and police intervened. Sheriffs fired high-velocity tear gas projectiles through the door of the cafe where Rubén and his friends had taken shelter. Rubén was killed when one of the projectiles hit him in the head.

Rubén Salazar grew up in the barrios of El Paso, Texas. He was able to experience first-hand the problems faced by Mexican Americans living in poor communities of the Southwest. These experiences made it possible for Rubén to write authentic newspaper articles about Mexican Americans.

Rubén Salazar died trying to get the facts for a story he was doing on Mexican Americans. There is now a Rubén Salazar Park in East Los Angeles and a CORRIDO (ballad) written in his honor. Mexican Americans are proud of Rubén Salazar because he was a talented, courageous journalist who tried to tell the truth about what he saw. His early death brought to an end a very promising journalistic career.

CHICANO (chee-cah-no)
RUBEN SALAZAR (roo-ben   sahl-ah-sahr)
CORRIDO (cor-ree-do)

GA1324

Who is a Chicano? And What is it the Chicanos Want?

A Chicano is a Mexican-American with a non-Anglo image of himself.

He resents being told Columbus "discovered" America when the Chicano's ancestors, the Mayans and the Aztecs, founded highly sophisticated civilizations centuries before Spain financed the Italian explorer's trip to the "New World."

Chicanos resent also Anglo pronouncements that Chicanos are "culturally deprived" or that the fact that they speak Spanish is a "problem."

Chicanos will tell you that their culture predates that of the Pilgrims and that Spanish was spoken in America before English and so the "problem" is not theirs but the Anglo's who don't speak Spanish.

Having told you that, the Chicano will then contend that Anglos are Spanish-oriented at the expense of Mexicans.

They will complain that when the governor dresses up as a Spanish nobleman for the Santa Barbara Fiesta he's insulting Mexicans because the Spanish conquered and exploited the Mexicans.

It's as if the governor dressed like an English Redcoat for the Fourth of July parade, Chicanos say.

When you think you know what Chicanos are getting at, a Mexican-American will tell you that Chicano is an insulting term and may even quote the Spanish Academy to prove that Chicano derives from chicanery.

A Chicano will scoff at this and say that such Mexican-Americans have been brainwashed by Anglos and that they're Tio Tacos (Uncle Toms). This type of Mexican Americans, Chicanos will argue, don't like the word Chicano because it's abrasive to their Anglo-oriented minds.

These poor people are brown Anglos, Chicanos will smirk.

What, then, is a Chicano? Chicanos say that if you have to ask you'll never understand, much less become a Chicano.

Actually, the word Chicano is as difficult to define as "Soul."

Such explanations, however, tend to miss the whole point as to why Mexican-American activists call themselves Chicanos.

Mexican-Americans, the second largest minority in the country and the largest in the Southwestern states (California, Texas, Arizona, New Mexico and Colorado), have always had difficulty making up their minds what to call themselves.

In New Mexico they call themselves Spanish-Americans. In other parts of the Southwest they call themselves Americans of Mexican descent, people with Spanish surnames or Hispanos.

Chicanos are trying to explain why not. Mexican-Americans, though indigenous to the Southwest, are on the lowest rung scholastically, economically, socially and politically. Chicanos feel cheated. They want to effect change. Now.

Mexican-Americans average eight years of schooling compared to the Negroes' 10 years. Farm workers, most of whom are Mexican-American in the Southwest, are excluded from the National Labor Relations Act unlike other workers. Also, Mexican-Americans often have to compete for low-paying jobs with their Mexican brothers from across the border who are willing to work for less. Mexican-Americans have to live with the stinging fact that the word Mexican is the synonym for inferior in many parts of the Southwest.

That is why Mexican-American activists flaunt the barrio word Chicano—as an act of defiance and a badge of honor. Mexican-Americans, though large in numbers, are so politically impotent that in Los Angeles, where the country's largest single concentration of Spanish-speaking live, they have no one of their own on the City Council. This, in a city politically sophisticated enough to have three Negro councilmen.

Chicanos, then, are merely fighting to become "Americans" Yes, but with a Chicano outlook.

By Rubén Salazar

What do Chicanos say about Mexicans?_____

_____

How do Chicanos feel about Columbus? _____

_____

What were the problems Chicanos faced in 1970? _____

_____

What has changed since this article was written in 1970? _____

_____

BARRIO BOY

ERNESTO GALARZA
"Man for All Seasons"
Teacher, Labor Expert,
Writer, Sociologist
1905-1984

ERNESTO GALARZA can be known as a "man for all seasons" because he excelled in many different fields. Dr. Galarza made important contributions to American education, farm labor, sociology and writing. During his life he worked as a teacher and a professor, giving many lectures to college students throughout the United States.

Dr. Galarza was also research director for the National Farm Labor Union and remained involved with the problems of farm workers for much of his life. From his experiences with farm workers, Dr. Galarza wrote many books on agricultural labor. Two of his most important are *Merchants of Labor: The Mexican Bracero Story* (1964) and *Spiders in the House and Workers in the Field* (1970), which tells the story of the farm workers' struggle to be recognized as a union and their defeat at the hands of powerful agribusiness.

His novel *Barrio Boy* (1971) tells the story of his early life in the mountain village of Jalcocotan near Tepic, Mexico, and his family's migration to a barrio in the United States during the Mexican Revolution. In his book, Dr. Galarza talks about how his family tries to stay together as a family, despite the many obstacles they encounter, and about what it was like for a young boy from a small village in Mexico to live in the United States.

Ernesto Galarza also enjoyed writing stories and poems for children in both Spanish and English. They were used in bilingual education programs. *ZOO RISA* and *RIMAS TONTINAS* are among some of his books for young children.

Dr. Galarza was orphaned during his youth by the death of his family. After this event he supported himself by doing odd jobs. In spite of these setbacks, Dr. Galarza obtained a college degree from Stanford University and later his doctorate from Columbia University. Dr. Galarza, who could have excelled in any profession, devoted his efforts to bringing attention to issues of injustice in agriculture and emphasizing the need to establish better education programs for Mexican American children.

BARRIO (bahr-ree-o)
ERNESTO GALARZA (ehr-nes-toh gah-lahr-zah)
RISA (rees-ah)
RIMAS TONTINAS (ree-mahs tohn-teen-ahs)

GA1324

RIMAS

Ernesto Galarza wrote in many styles and much of what he wrote was for children.

He wrote short poems in Spanish and in English versions called poemas pequeñitos, or short poems. Then he wrote even shorter poems of four lines, which appeared in the booklet *Poems, Peque peque puequeñitos*.

Here are examples.

No abraces a Mariquita. La apachurras. Pobrecita.	Never hug a Ladybug. She is agile, Oh so fragile.

Que tontería buscar la luna al mediodía.	Don't look for the moon on a sunny day. You won't find it anyway.

Ernesto Galarza, Colleccion Mini-Libros, 1974.
Reprinted with permission.

Take an idea and write a short poem of four lines like this in English or in Spanish.

_____

_____

_____

_____

RUDOLFO ANAYA
Writer
1937

TOMAS RIVERA
Writer
1935-1984

Scholars, poets and writers have played important roles in the lives of Mexican Americans. Education has been an important part of this development. As early as 1542, approximately one hundred years before Harvard University was established in the United States, Mexico established a university.

Because the Southwest was a frontier with little access to metropolitan areas, myths, legends and oral traditions became part of the new way of life of the people. Many of their stories and poems were passed from one generation to another through the oral tradition. It was not unusual for poets to recite their poems at social gatherings. People relied heavily on the spoken word and even children were taught to recite long epic poems.

Also, in the early days, all of the writing done by Mexican Americans was done in Spanish, and publishers were not interested in publishing Spanish works. Thus it was difficult for Mexican American writers to get their material published. There presently exists more opportunities for this material to be published because Mexican American writers and poets are now writing in English or bilingually.

TOMAS RIVERA and RUDOLFO ANAYA are two writers whose works have been published extensively. Tomás Rivera's book *¡Y NO SE LO TRAGO LA TIERRA!*, translated to mean "and the earth did not part," reflects the many experiences Mexican Americans have undergone in the United States. This book of short stories, which is more like a novel with its theme of struggle for survival, is free of stereotypes. The authentic characters in these stories reflect what Mexican Americans do, think and feel much more accurately than do those of any other writer.

The novelist Rudolfo Anaya, who began to write when he was still a child and is still writing extensively, has written a brilliant novel, *Bless Me, Ultima*, which has been printed and reprinted many times. The novel, set in New Mexico, is the story of the life of a young Mexican American boy and the important role that the old one, ULTIMA, plays in the life of the people.

Both of these skilled writers write about the things they know and have lived, and this gives their writing a quality of authority and authenticity. In the past, many things have been written about Mexican Americans and their way of life, which, when read by the Mexican American people, seem to be filled with stereotypes and distortions. Writers who write in this manner have little understanding of the people they are writing about, and while they may have good intentions, their writing reflects their misunderstanding. Good writers must always be sure of their facts.

AUTORES (ah-oo-tohr-es)
TOMAS RIVERA (toh-mahs ree-vay-rah)
RUDOLFO ANAYA (roo-dohl-foh ah-nay-ya)
Y NO SE LO TRAGO LA TIERRA (ee no say loh tray-goh lah tee-ahr-ah)
ULTIMA (oohl-tee-mah)

GA1324

WRITERS

RUDOLFO ACUÑA (ah-coon-ya) was born in Los Angeles, California, during the Depression. He was an author and professor of Mexican American history. His best-known work is *Occupied America: The Chicano's Struggle Toward Liberation* (1972).

ALBERTO URISTA HEREDIA ALURISTA (ah-loo-rees-ta) was born in Mexico City, but raised in Los Angeles. He is a poet and active in Mexican American causes. He was considered a leading Chicano poet in the 1960's and explored Chicano themes, often mixing Spanish and English. One of his poems is "La Cara de Mi Padre."

JOSE ANTONIO BURCIAGA (boor-cee-ah-gah) was born in Texas. He is both a writer and an artist, often using humor, such as his *We De Peepo*.

ABELARDO BARRIENTOS DELGADO (dayl-gah-do) was born in Mexico and raised in Texas. He moved about the Southwest as a community organizer, taught at universities and wrote over one thousand poems. One of his publications was *Chicano: 25 Pieces of a Chicano Mind* (1969).

IGNACIO E. LOZANO, SR., (loh-sah-no) was born in Mexico and raised in Texas. In 1913 he began publishing a Spanish weekly newspaper, *La Prensa*. In 1926 he began another newspaper, *La Opinion*, in Los Angeles.

AMERICO PAREDES (pah-ray-des) was born in Texas and became a great scholar of Mexican American history. He served in the U.S. army as a correspondent and taught at the University of Texas in El Paso. He wrote a history called *With His Pistol in His Hand: A Border Ballad and Its Hero* in 1958.

TOMAS RIVERA (ree-vay-rah) was born in Texas to an immigrant family. He pursued an education in Spanish literature and wrote many novels, as well as teaching in several universities. He became the first Mexican American chancellor of the University of California at Riverside. When he died of a heart attack in 1984, a Tomás Rivera Center for Mexican American Studies was started in his honor at the university. His best-known novel is *¡Y No se lo Tragó la Tierra!*

OCTAVIO ROMANO (roh-mah-noh) was born in Mexico and grew up in New Mexico. He received a doctorate degree in anthropology and became a supporter of Chicano literature by starting Quinto Sol Publications in 1967 and later a journal called *El Grito*.

GARY SOTO (soh-toh) was born and raised in California. He is a poet and professor of Chicano Studies at Berkeley. His poems and stories talk about the Mexican American experience, as in his *Living Up the Street* (1989).

JOSE ANTONIO VILLARREAL (vee-ah-ree-ahl) was born in California and taught in the United States and Mexico. His best-known novel is *Pocho* (1959).

GA1324

BOOKS

Fill in the names of the authors for the books and publications below. When the title is in Spanish, select the title from the box below that you think is probably the translation in English.

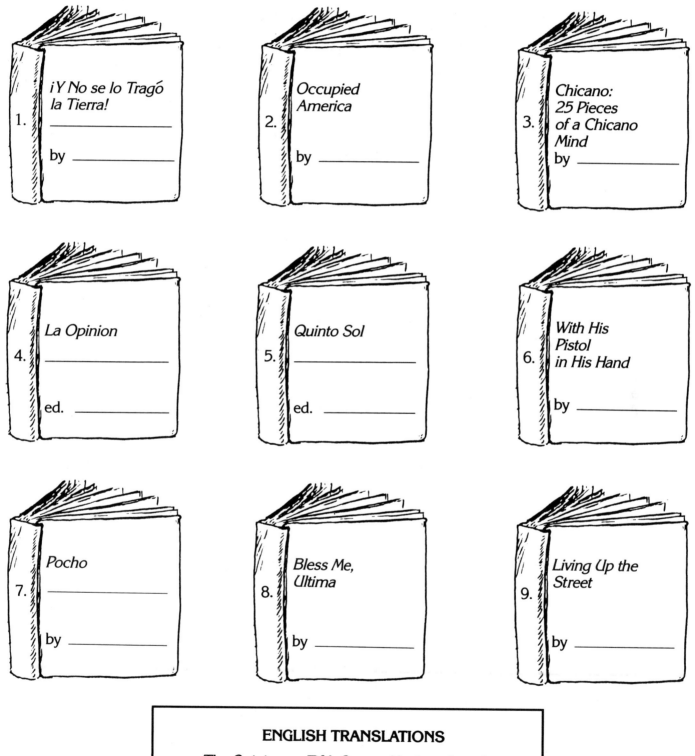

1. ¡Y No se lo Tragó la Tierra!

_____

by _____

2. Occupied America

by _____

3. Chicano: 25 Pieces of a Chicano Mind

by _____

4. La Opinion

_____

ed. _____

5. Quinto Sol

_____

ed. _____

6. With His Pistol in His Hand

by _____

7. Pocho

_____

by _____

8. Bless Me, Ultima

by _____

9. Living Up the Street

by _____

ENGLISH TRANSLATIONS

*The Opinion   Fifth Sun   Mexican American
And the Earth Did Not Part*

EDUCADOR

GEORGE I. SANCHEZ
JORGE ISIDORO SANCHEZ Y SANCHEZ
Educational Pioneer and Man of Courage
1906-1972

JORGE ISIDORO SANCHEZ Y SANCHEZ, better known as George I. Sánchez, is often referred to as the most outstanding Mexican American scholar. He is also known as a leader who was forceful and courageous and as a man who always put the interests of people first.

George Sánchez was born in New Mexico to a family of early day New Mexican settlers. His ancestors helped to colonize New Mexico in the seventeenth century. Some of George's early years were spent growing up in a rough mining town in Arizona, where his father worked as a miner.

As a young man, George loved learning, and in the summers when he wasn't working as a teacher, he attended college. When he was only seventeen, he got his first job teaching in a one-room school. Later he became a principal. Still wanting more education, George attended the University of California at Berkeley on a scholarship, and in 1934 he received a Doctorate in Education.

He became a professor at the University of Texas and had a long career in teaching, research and writing. Dr. Sánchez's most famous book is *Forgotten People*, a study of the Mexican American people of New Mexico. He became an expert on the education of the Spanish-speaking people in the United States.

Many things that Dr. Sánchez saw troubled him. His biggest concern was the education of Mexican American children, and as early as the year 1934, he was talking about the high dropout rate among Mexican American school children. He spoke out against injustice and ignorance toward Mexican Americans and questioned whether a standardized test of intelligence could measure the intelligence of Mexican American children. He also studied how segregated schools affected Mexican American children and spoke out against discrimination and segregation.

George Sánchez knew about his history and was very proud of his Indian, Spanish and Mexican roots. He saw the Spanish lanugage as the heritage of Mexican American children and was quick to remind people that in the sixteenth century in Mexico, children went to school and learned three languages: Spanish, Latin and NAHUATL with positive effects.

Today's bilingual education programs owe a lot to the early work of George Sánchez. He believed that bilingual programs could be the basis for better understanding among people of different cultures, as well as a way to assist Mexican American children with their education. His farsighted ideas, seldom acknowledged during his lifetime even among his colleagues at the university, had to wait many years before they would be accepted.

EDUCADOR (e-doo-cah-dor)
JORGE ISIDORO SANCHEZ (hor-hay   ee-see-dor-o   sahn-chez)
NAHUATL (nah-oo-ah-tl)

67

GA1324

DISCRIMINATION AND SEGREGATION

Imagine you did not understand English and school was all in English.

How long do you think it would take you to learn English? What would you be able to understand in your classes? How well would you do on the tests?

The prefix *bi-* means "two." *Bilingual* means "two _____" and *bicultural* means "two _____." What are the advantages of knowing another language? What other languages would you like to know? What do you think *culture* is?

The reading mentions two conditions that George Sánchez spoke out against. One was discrimination and the other was segregation. Look up each of these words in a dictionary and write their definitions on the lines below. Then give an example of each.

discrimination: _____

_____

example of discrimination: _____

_____

_____

segregation: _____

_____

example of segregation: _____

_____

_____

Why do you think George Sánchez thought these were problems for Mexican American students?

GA1324

THE LEMON GROVE CASE

In the 1930's in Lemon Grove, California, the elementary schools were segregated. So were many other schools in the Southwest. Mexican American children attended a school on one side of town, and all the other children attended school on another side of town.

The teachers and members of the school board argued that it was for the best education of the children, because the children who could not speak English could be taught together and not only learn English but also "American" ways. These schools were sometimes called "Americanization" schools.

However, many of the Mexican American children who didn't speak Spanish, only English, were also assigned to these schools because they were Mexican American.

The parents of one sixth-grade boy at the Lemon Grove school, ROBERTO ALVAREZ, decided to speak out against what they felt was an unfair education their son was receiving. They formed a group of parents of Mexican American children, and together they decided to file a case in court.

The court decided in favor of the Alvarez family, and as a result, it became unlawful in California to segregate children by race or ethnic background.

A GROUP PROJECT

Take a survey of the students in your classroom.

    1. How many boys and girls are in the classroom?

    2. What languages does each of them speak?

    3. What is their ethnic or racial background?

Design a chart or graph which describes your classroom.

ROBERTO ALVAREZ (ro-<u>bayr</u>-to <u>ahl</u>-vah-res)

EDUCATORS

FRANK ANGEL, JR., (ahn-hayl) was born and raised in New Mexico. From 1972 to 1976 he became the first Mexican American president of a four-year college in the United States, the president of New Mexico Highlands University. He was followed as president by John Aragon from 1976 to 1984. Aragon received many awards, including the George I. Sánchez Award for improving cultural understanding.

TOMAS ARCINIEGA (ahr-see-nee-ay-gah) was born in Texas but pursued a career in education in California. He became the first Mexican American president in the California state colleges. He writes about bilingual education and Mexican American issues.

ATURO MADRID BARELA (bah-ray-lah) was born in New Mexico and became a scholar in languages and literature. He was also an administrator and taught at several universities. In 1975 he helped start the National Chicano Council on Higher Education.

CECILIA PRECIADO DE BURCIAGA (boor-see-ah-gah) was born in California and followed a career in education and teaching. She was appointed to a position with the U.S. government's Commission on Civil Rights and became a representative on many national groups for women's rights.

CARLOS CASTAÑEDA (cahs-tahn-yay-dah) was born in Mexico but grew up in Texas. After serving in the U.S. army, he pursued a career in history and became one of the leading authorities on Mexican history and culture in the Southwest.

LAURO CAVAZOS, JR., (cah-vah-soos) was born in Texas and studied sciences. He became president of Texas Tech University and was U.S. Secretary of Education from 1988 to 1990.

CARLOS CORTES (cohr-tes) was born in California and spent time in the army and studied journalism before becoming a leading historian of Latin American studies. He wrote many histories about Mexican Americans and sections about their history in encyclopedias.

JULIAN NAVA (nah-vah) was born in Los Angeles, California, to a migrant family. He served in the U.S. Air Force and went on to study and obtain a doctorate degree in history. He was an author of several school books on Mexican American history and served two terms on the Los Angeles School Board. President Carter named him Ambassador to Mexico.

JUAN GOMEZ QUIÑONES (keen-yohn-es) was born in Mexico but grew up in Los Angeles, California, and became a scholar and author of Latin American history and Director of the Chicano Research Center at U.C.L.A.

JULIAN SAMORA (sah-moh-rah) was born in Colorado and pursued his studies in sociology and anthropology, the study of man and society. He taught at Notre Dame and wrote a history called *La Raza: Forgotten Americans* in 1966.

GA1324

ACCOMPLISHMENTS

George Sánchez is one of the first of many educators in the Mexican American community, many of whom are also authors and have used their powers of teaching and writing to help examine the condition of Mexican Americans and the injustices they have faced.

Fill in the name of the educator who best fits each description below.

1. Director of the Chicano Research Center at the University of California in Los Angeles

   _____

2. First Mexican American president of a college in California

   _____

3. Appointed to a position with the U.S. Commission on Civil Rights

   _____

4. Named as an ambassador to Mexico

   _____

5. A scholar in the area of languages and literature

   _____

6. Wrote histories of Mexican Americans for sections in encyclopedias

   _____

7. First Mexican American president of a four-year college in the U.S.

   _____

8. Received the George I. Sánchez Award

   _____

9. A leading authority on Mexican history and the culture of the Southwest

   _____

10. Studied anthropology and sociology

   _____

11. Became a U.S. Secretary of Education

THE HERITAGE OF MEXICAN TEACHERS

In the city of Guadalajara, Mexico, there is a statue dedicated to teachers. It was made by collecting keys from school children all over the city and melting the iron, which was then molded by artists into the statue. It now stands as a monument to the efforts of Mexican teachers.

One of the most interesting things about the statue of the teacher is that it has two heads. One head represents the teaching side of the educator, and the other represents the effort of teachers to improve society.

Many Mexican American teachers follow careers in education, contributing to the better understanding and improvement of conditions for Mexican Americans in our society.

GA1324

MAESTRA

MARI LUCI JARAMILLO
Professor, Diplomat, Administrator
1928

MARI LUCI JARAMILLO is the first Mexican American woman to represent the United States as an ambassador. In 1977 President Jimmy Carter appointed her as Ambassador to Honduras.

Mari Luci grew up in New Mexico, where she attended school. It was during the time of the Great Depression. Despite having to work through four years of college, Mari Luci still managed to graduate *magna cum laude*, which means "with high honors." She became a teacher and learned many things about Mexican American children from working with them. Among the things Mari Luci learned was that she could teach these children better if she incorporated things they were familiar with into her lessons. Later, using her methods, she was able to help many classroom teachers who also worked with Mexican American children.

Still desiring more education, Mari Luci attended the University of New Mexico at Albuquerque, and in 1979 she received her Doctorate of Education. She became a professor and later head of the Department of Elementary Education. Because of her knowledge about education and her writings in professional journals, she was invited to give many speeches before large audiences. She inspired all who came to hear her speak.

All this activity led to many honors. In 1973 McGraw Hill Broadcasting Company named her Outstanding Chicana of the Year. Mari Luci received the New Mexico Distinguished Service Award in 1977, and in 1985 she was appointed the Chairwoman of the Tomás Rivera Center, a national institute for policy studies. She also took the position of Regional Director for the Educational Testing Service.

Although Mari Luci Jaramillo has held many important positions, she has never forgotten her work with Mexican American children, and she continues to write articles about her favorite topic—making education better for bilingual children.

MAESTRA (mahy-<u>ays</u>-tra)
MARI LUCI JARAMILLO (<u>mahr</u>-ree loo-see hah-rah-<u>mee</u>-yo)

GA1324

MAESTRA

Mari Lucy Jaramillo has won many awards as an educator, a teacher and a professor. She is an excellent example of the Spanish word *maestra*.

In Mexico, every year since 1917, the students in schools honor their teachers on May 15, which is El Dia del Maestro—the Day of the Teacher. On that day, students bring flowers or fruit and write poems and speeches for their teachers. This custom was recently imported to the Southwest, where on a designated day in May, schools celebrate the Day of the Teacher. It was originated in California in 1982 by the Association of Mexican American Educators, and that state was the first to have an official Day of the Teacher.

Does your state or school celebrate a Day of the Teacher?

DON'T WAIT! Honor your teacher by writing a short poem or thank-you message. Decorate it as a poster or a card.

 GA1324

SIGN LANGUAGE

Mari Luci was especially concerned about students who didn't know English and couldn't understand what was going on in their classrooms. She was one of the first educators to advocate for students being taught in their own language while they were learning English.

Imagine what it would be like not to understand the language around you and not to be able to read signs or follow directions.

Below are some signs in Spanish. Try to match each with its English translation.

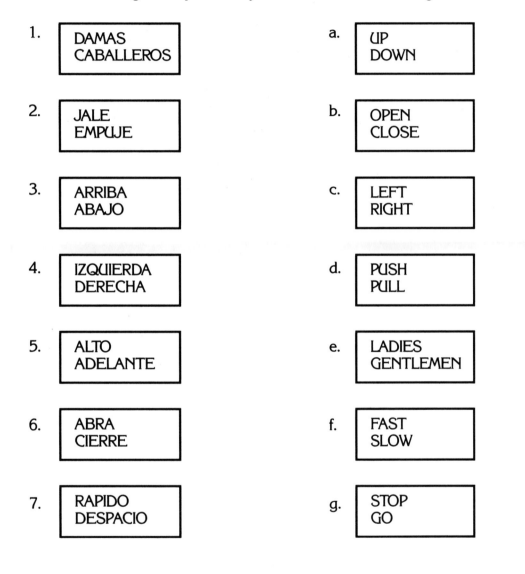

1. DAMAS
   CABALLEROS

2. JALE
   EMPUJE

3. ARRIBA
   ABAJO

4. IZQUIERDA
   DERECHA

5. ALTO
   ADELANTE

6. ABRA
   CIERRE

7. RAPIDO
   DESPACIO

a. UP
   DOWN

b. OPEN
   CLOSE

c. LEFT
   RIGHT

d. PUSH
   PULL

e. LADIES
   GENTLEMEN

f. FAST
   SLOW

g. STOP
   GO

DAMAS (dah-mahs)
CABALLEROS (cah-bah-ya-ros)
JALE (ha-lay)
EMPUJE (em-poo-hay)
ARRIBA (ahr-ree-bah)
ABAJO (ah-bah-ho)
IZQUIERDA (ees-kee-ayr-dah)

DERECHO (day-ray-cho)
ALTO (ahl-to)
ADELANTE (ah-day-lahn-tay)
ABRA (ah-brah)
CIERRE (see-ahr-ray)
RAPIDO (rah-pee-do)
DESPACIO (des-pah-see-o)

GA1324

AMBASSADORS

In groups of four or five, find out about ambassadors. Take notes.

1. How are ambassadors selected? Where could you look to find out? Begin by listing three possible places.

   a. _____

   b. _____

   c. _____

2. What do ambassadors do? What do they do for the countries they represent? What do they do in the countries to which they are assigned?

   _____

   _____

   _____

3. Who is the present-day ambassador to Honduras? To Mexico?

   Honduras: _____

   Mexico: _____

4. Does an ambassador need to speak the language of the country to which he is assigned? Do you think Mari Luci could speak the language of Honduras?

   _____

   If you were selected as an ambassador, to what country would you like to be assigned and why?

   _____

   _____

   _____

   _____

   _____

Discuss your answers from the notes you took.

MUJER

GLORIA MOLINA
Politician, Activist
1948

It was a history-making day in 1982 when GLORIA MOLINA was elected. She was the first Mexican American woman in the California State Assembly. In 1984 she again ran for the same seat and won. While on the State Assembly, she was known as a strong leader. Powerful legislators thought twice before they challenged her. They knew she studied the issues very carefully and would not back down easily from a position she believed in. She always championed the rights of children and the poor. She spoke for individuals who had no voice in government.

Gloria Molina was the first Mexican American woman to hold an important legislative position in California. In 1987 Gloria decided to run for a position on the Los Angeles City Council rather than continue as a member of the California State Assembly. Again, she was the first Mexican American woman in the history of that city elected to sit on one of the most powerful city council positions in the United States.

Born to parents who immigrated from Mexico, Gloria was the oldest of ten children in her family. She grew up and went to school in Pico Rivera, California, and attended East Los Angeles City College. Growing up was not easy for Gloria. When she was nineteen, her father had a serious accident, and she became the only source of support for her family. In order to finish college she had to work during the day as a legal assistant and attend school at night.

There was always a part of Gloria that fought for the rights of people, and in 1973 she became the founding president of the COMISION FEMENIL DE LOS ANGELES (Women's Commission of Los Angeles). As president of the Comisión, Gloria Molina helped to develop many social service programs which assist Mexican American women from being exploited in work, housing, health and immigration. She also helped initiate other Latino political organizations.

Back in 1974 Gloria Molina became Administrative Assistant to California Assemblyman ART TORRES. Three years later she was selected by President Jimmy Carter as Regional Director of Intergovernmental and Congressional Affairs in the Department of Health, Education and Welfare. In 1980 Gloria became Chief Deputy to Willie Brown, Speaker of the California State Assembly.

Added to her list of accomplishments and honors are 1984 *MS.* magazine's Woman of the Year award, MALDEF's Valerie Kantor Woman of Achievement Award and *CAMINOS* magazine's 1983 Woman of the Year award. Gloria Molina is a fine example of the woman's fighting spirit and determination, in the face of great odds against her, to accomplish her goals and those of her family and community.

MUJER (moo-hayr)
GLORIA MOLINA (moh-lee-nah)
COMISION FEMENIL (coh-mee-see-ohn   fay-may-neel)
ART TORRES (tor-rays)
CAMINOS (cah-mee-nos)

GA1324

POLITICIAN AND COMMUNITY ACTIVIST

Gloria Molina is a *politician* and a *community activist*. What do each of these words mean? What is the difference between them, and how does one receive these titles or positions?

politician: _____

_____

community activist: _____

_____

Gloria served in federal, state and city government positions. From the reading, what position did she hold in each?

Federal (Washington, D.C.): _____

State (California): _____

City (Los Angeles): _____

From the biography, write in the awards or titles Gloria Molina received in the following years:

1973 _____

1974 _____

1980 _____

1982 _____

1983 _____

1984 _____

1987 _____

PATHFINDER

Gloria was the first in her family and community to do many things, a *pathfinder*.

Find other women who have been the first to do something in your family or community. Choose one woman to interview. Ask questions such as: How old were you at the time? Who encouraged you? Who were your role models? What did you have to do to reach your goal?

MS. _____

The first to _____

_____

_____

_____

_____

_____

_____

_____

_____

_____

_____

_____

_____

_____

_____

_____

_____

_____

_____

_____

_____

Bring a picture of your pathfinder to put with the essay for a class display.

GA1324

GOBERNADOR

TONEY ANAYA
Politician
1941

When TONEY ANAYA became governor of New Mexico from 1983 to 1986, he was the only Mexican American governor in the entire United States. As governor, Anaya's concerns focused on the low voter turnout of Mexican Americans, poverty and the alarming drop-out rate among Hispanic students. He felt that Mexican American people should involve themselves in improving their own conditions, and that they should have a clear understanding of the role of government and the important issues facing them. During his term as governor, he held national meetings to discuss these issues and to develop strong organizations to work on these problems.

Toney Anaya was no stranger to poverty. He was the seventh of ten children of a New Mexican cowboy and grew up in a three-room adobe house with dirt floors and no plumbing or electricity. His parents, who had little education themselves, stressed the importance of education to their children, and Toney attended New Mexico Highlands University on a scholarship.

Always interested in politics, Toney Anaya worked for Senator Dennis Chávez in Washington, D.C., while he finished his law degree at the Washington College of Law, American University. Still later, he worked for Senator Joseph Montoya of New Mexico as his legislative counsel. After being admitted to the bar, Toney Anaya became Administrative Assistant to New Mexico's Governor Bruce King. In 1974 he ran for attorney general of New Mexico and won, and in 1982 he ran for governor of New Mexico and won.

Toney Anaya was a forceful and courageous governor who was not afraid to support issues that were near and dear to the hearts of the poor and to the quality of life for all of the people in the United States. He was a strong governor who could probably have had a second term as governor if New Mexico's law did not prohibit a governor from succeeding himself.

GOBERNADOR (goh-ber-nah-<u>dor</u>)
ANAYA (ah-<u>nahy</u>-yah)

MEXICAN AMERICAN POLITICIANS AND LEADERS

JERRY APODOCA (ah-po-<u>dah</u>-cah) was governor of New Mexico in 1975.

RAMONA ACOSTA BAÑUELOS (bahn-<u>way</u>-los), a businesswoman, was appointed U.S. Treasurer from 1971 to 1974.

POLLY BACA BARRAGAN (bahr-rah-<u>gan</u>) was elected in 1974 to the Colorado State House of Representatives and then to the Colorado Senate in 1978.

RAUL CASTRO (<u>cas</u>-troh) became the first Mexican American governor of Arizona in 1974. He also served as Ambassador to Bolivia (1968-1970) and Argentina (1977-1980).

DENNIS CHAVEZ (<u>cha</u>-ves) was a U.S. senator from New Mexico, reelected five times and serving from 1935 to 1962. He was known for his support of civil rights and education.

HENRY CISNEROS (sees-<u>ner</u>-ohs) was elected mayor of San Antonio, Texas, in 1981.

BERT CORONA (co-<u>rohn</u>-ah) was a political activist and Texas labor organizer, especially involved in immigration issues and bias in the media.

HENRY GONZALES (gohn-<u>sahl</u>-es) was the first Texan of Mexican descent in the U.S. House of Representatives and then was elected U.S. senator in 1961. He is interested primarily in civil rights, housing and benefits.

RODOLFO "CORKY" GONZALES (gohn-<u>sahl</u>-es) was a Chicano leader in Colorado in the 1960's and 1970's. He led the Chicano contingent in the Poor People's March on Washington and organzied the Colorado Raza Unida Party. He is also known for his poem, "I Am Joaquín," a statement about Chicano identity.

JOSE ANGEL GUTIERREZ (goo-tee-<u>ahr</u>-es) was an educator and then judge in Texas. He organized MAYO, Mexican American Youth Organization, and helped create the La Raza Unida Party in Texas.

MANUEL LUJAN, JR., (<u>loo</u>-hahn) was elected to the U.S. House of Representatives from New Mexico in 1968 and was appointed U.S. Secretary of the Interior in 1984.

JOSEPH M. MONTOYA (mohn-<u>toy</u>-yah) was elected to the U.S. House of Representatives in 1964 and served until 1976. He was an advocate for the poor.

KATHERINE D. ORTEGA (ohr-<u>tay</u>-gah), a businesswoman, was appointed U.S. Treasurer in 1983.

FEDERICO PEÑA (<u>payn</u>-yah) was a state legislator in Colorado and then became the mayor of Denver in 1984.

EDWARD R. ROYBAL (roy-<u>bahl</u>) served thirteen years on the City Council of Los Angeles and was elected to the U.S. Congress in 1962. He introduced the first bilingual education act in 1967.

ESTEBAN TORRES (<u>toh</u>-res) served several federal appointments, including ambassador, and was elected in 1982 to the U.S. House of Representatives.

REYES LOPES TIJERINA (tee-hay-ree-na) was a leader and activist in the 1960's. He moved from Texas with his followers to New Mexico and worked on restoring Mexican land grants. By mid 1960 he had twenty thousand followers.

BANDIDOS
Folk Heroes

Stripped of all their possessions and land and treated as intruders, some Mexican Americans in the second half of the nineteenth century took to carrying out raids on Anglo-Americans. Their resistance to unjust treatment brought about a period of banditry. These individuals were regarded as outlaws by the Anglo-Americans, but by the Mexican American population, some were considered folk heroes. The reaction by the Anglo-American community was often to retaliate by lynching Mexican Americans.

JUAN NEPOMUCENO CORTINA (cohr-tee-nah) was a rancher in 1859 involved in a Texas dispute where he protected an employee against the marshal. He fled to Mexico and organized followers who volunteered to right some of the injustices, but produced a backlash of hatred against Mexicans. He joined the Mexican struggle against the French in the 1860's and died in Mexico. He was a center of controversy and a product of his times.

GREGORIO CORTEZ LIRA (cohr-tes) was accused of killing a sheriff in Texas in 1901. There was a misunderstanding over a horse theft, and he actually shot in self-defense. He became a legend when he evaded a posse of three hundred men for ten days before he was captured. His story has been the subject of Mexican corridos and also a movie starring Edward James Olmos. He became the symbol of the injustices to Mexicans in Texas and resistance to that injustice.

JOAQUIN MURRIETA (moor-ree-ay-tah) was one of many Mexican or Californio miners driven off the mines in the Gold Rush. He became an outlaw and was one of the famous five Joaquíns, all with the first name of Joaquín. Rangers were organized to capture the bandits and Joaquín was killed along with another famous bandit, Three Fingered Jack. The head of Joaquín and hand of the other bandit were cut off and put in jars of alcohol to become part of touring shows. Joaquín was a product of the injustices of the times and became a legend and symbol to the Californios of resistance. Some of the aspects of Cisco the Kid and Zorro were based on the life of Joaquín Murrieta.

TIBURCIO VASQUEZ (vahs-kez) was involved in the killing of a constable at a dance and fled to avoid being lynched. He was arrested in 1857 for horse stealing, put in prison and then escaped. In 1875 he was finally caught and hanged. He was also a symbol of the injustices done to Mexican Americans in early California.

GA1324

HEROES

WAR HEROES

Among the many contributions Mexican Americans have made to the United States has been their valiant efforts during times of war. They have served in all of the wars, including World War I, World War II, Korea and Vietnam, often giving their lives for their country.

Between 350,000 and 500,000 Mexican Americans fought in World War II. They won thirty-nine Congressional Medals of Honor, making them the most decorated of any minority group in the United States. Medals are awarded for great deeds of bravery and the Congressional Medal of Honor is the highest military award given by the United States.

Two men who serve as examples of individuals receiving this award are Private JOSE P. MARTINEZ and RODOLFO HERNANDEZ. Private Martinez of Colorado won the Congressional Medal of Honor in the war in the Pacific, when he single-handedly cleared a pass of enemy soldiers. He lost his life in the process.

Rodolfo Hernandez from California enlisted into the army when he was only seventeen years old as a way to support his mother and other members of his family. It was during the Korean conflict, and Rodolfo Hernandez became cut off from his unit. He ran out of ammunition and ended up in hand-to-hand combat with the enemy. He kept the enemy from advancing against his unit, but as a result of his brave act, he received serious head injuries.

In spite of the bravery of these individuals and others like them, their acts of heroism have gone unrecognized. These Mexican Americans who have proven themselves in battle have often encountered discrimination upon their return to their home communities.

One community in Silvis, Illinois, decided to change this state of affairs. There is now a street in this small town by the name of Hero Street. It was named by the people of the community to honor their own Mexican American war heroes.

HEROES (ayr-oh-es)
JOSE MARTINEZ (hoh-say   mahr-teen-es)
RODOLFO HERNANDEZ (roh-dohl-foh   ayr-nahn-days)

GA1324

MEXICAN AMERICANS IN SPORTS

ROBERT CHACON (cha-cohn) was born in 1952 in Los Angeles. In 1974 he became the World Featherweight Champion of boxing.

TOM FLORES (flohr-ays) was born in 1937 in California. He became a football quarterback with the Oakland Raiders from 1960 to 1966 and with the Buffalo Bills from 1967 to 1969. In 1979 he became the head coach for the Los Angeles Raiders and led them to a Super Bowl victory in 1984.

RICHARD ALONSO (PANCHO) GONZALES (gohn-sahl-ays) was born in 1928 in Los Angeles. He became a star player of tennis from 1955 to 1970. In 1966 he won the World Championship at Wembley, England, and in 1971 the Pacific Southwest Tournament. When he retired he coached tennis and owned a tennis ranch.

NANCY LOPEZ (loh-pes) was born in 1957 in California. In 1977 she joined the Ladies Professional Golf Association, the LPGA. She was named Player of the Year, Female Athlete of the Year and Pro-Golf Player of the Year in 1979. In 1987 she qualified for the LPGA Hall of Fame by winning her thirty-fifth tournament. She became interested in golf by following her parents on the golf course when she was eight years old. Her followers and supporters are known as Nancy's Navy.

CARLOS PALOMINO (cahr-los pah-lo-mee-no) was born in 1950 in Mexico but grew up in Southern California. He took up boxing in the army, and by the time he left the military he was the World Military Champion. He became a professional boxer in 1972. In 1976 he won the World Welterweight title of boxing. He retired in 1979.

JAMES PLUNKETT was born in 1947 in California. He played football while he was a student at Stanford University. Later he played football for the New England Patriots, the San Francisco Forty-Niners and the Los Angeles Raiders. He was one of the star players for the Raiders in the Super Bowl in 1981 and again in 1984.

LEE TREVIÑO (tray-veen-yo) was born in 1939 in Texas. He grew up in a house next to a golf course. After serving in the Marine Corps, he entered the professional world of golf by winning the U.S. Open in 1968. In 1971 he was the first golfer to win both the U.S. Canadian Open and the British Open golf tournaments in the same year. In 1981 he was named to the World Golf Hall of Fame, and in 1984 he won the PGA (Professional Golf Association) Championship. His followers are known as Lee's Fleas.

DANNY VILLANUEVA (vee-yah-noo-way-vah) was born in 1937 in New Mexico. He played football in college and became a professional player for the Los Angeles Rams from 1960 to 1964. He was traded to the Dallas Cowboys and played with them for the next three years and then retired from football. He became a businessman in Los Angeles and vice president of the Spanish language television station.

GA1324

CHAMPIONS

Fill in the name of the sports champion next to his/her achievement.

1. Coached the winning team in the 1984 Super Bowl _____

2. World Welterweight Champion in 1976 _____

3. Played with the Dallas Cowboys _____

4. Made the World Golf Hall of Fame in 1981 _____

5. World Featherweight Champion in 1974 _____

6. Made the LPGA Hall of Fame in 1987 _____

7. Star player for the Los Angeles Raiders _____

8. Won the World Championship of Tennis in 1966 _____

GA1324

CALAVERA

EL DIA DE LOS MUERTOS
Day of the Dead
November 1 and 2

In many places of the Southwest, people of Mexican descent still observe and celebrate a unique Mexican holiday called EL DIA DE LOS MUERTOS, or Day of the Dead. This is a custom that many native peoples in Mexico observed before the Spaniards came and is a holiday that takes place in the fall. The native peoples believed that on that day the spirits of family members who have died are allowed to return from their afterlife to visit the family. Although they cannot be seen nor heard, they will take comfort in knowing they are remembered.

In order to celebrate the holiday, an ALTAR is built in the home. The altar is made from tables and boxes in the shape of a pyramid and decorated with a tablecloth, traditional items, food and articles which belonged to the person who died. People often decorate their altar with paper cutouts called PAPEL PICADO, candles, skeleton toys and sugar candies made in the shape of skulls. Fresh fruits and vegetables, favorite foods and something to drink are also left overnight on the altar.

The belief is that those who have died visit on the evening of November 1. The family prays and burns candles to "light the way" for the spirit. It is said tears will only make the spirit's path slippery. The next day, El Dia de los Muertos, the family and relatives come together for a meal. After the holiday is over, the altar is taken down. In some towns in Mexico, the family goes to the cemetery and celebrates the holiday at the gravesites.

Besides the serious side of El Dia de los Muertos, there are many humorous customs. This is very much a holiday for children. The markets in Mexico have many toys for children made of wood in the form of skeletons which dance and do tricks. There are also candies in the form of sugar skulls, with names written across their foreheads, that children buy to give to their friends, similar to our custom of chocolate-covered Easter eggs or valentine candy hearts.

This holiday takes place just a day after Halloween and at first seems to be like Halloween with all the skeleton images. But it is not scary like Halloween. Children don't dress up in costumes, and the skeletons are more like clowns. El Dia de los Muertos is a time to remember that death will come to everyone.

CALAVERA (ca-lah-vay-rah)
EL DIA DE LOS MUERTOS (el dee-ah day los moo-er-tos)
ALTAR (ahl-tahr)
PAPEL PICADO (pah-pel pee-cah-do)

THE TRADITION OF DAY OF THE DEAD

In groups of four or five, compare the Mexican tradition of El Dia de los Muertos to Halloween.

In what ways are they alike?

1. _____

2. _____

3. _____

In what ways are they different?

1. _____

2. _____

3. _____

What does El Dia de los Muertos have in common with these other holidays?

Christmas _____

_____

Valentine's Day _____

_____

Memorial Day _____

_____

Easter _____

_____

Thanksgiving _____

_____

A popular joke tells about the Mexican who took food to the grave of his wife. In the same cemetery, another man was taking flowers for his wife's grave. The second man said to the Mexican, "When is your dead one going to come up to eat the food?" The first man replied, "When yours comes up to smell the flowers."

What is the message of this joke?

GA1324

DROP DEAD

English has many expressions containing the word *dead*. A few of them are illustrated on this page.

In groups of four or five, brainstorm and come up with as many expressions as you can that contain the word *dead*, and illustrate them like the ones on this page. This kind of humor is similar to the Mexican humor for Day of the Dead.

Expressions with the word *dead*.

GA1324

CINCO DE MAYO

Mexican Americans, like all Mexicans, prize their freedom and have struggled throughout their history to remain free. An important holiday that commemorates their struggle for independence is CINCO DE MAYO. It is called the Fifth of May because it was on this day in 1862 that the Mexican people showed their uncommon courage by defeating a better-equipped French army. This French army of six thousand soldiers commanded by General Lawrencez had never been defeated and fully expected to defeat the four thousand poorly equipped Mexican soldiers headed by General IGNACIO ZARAGOZA. The French scorned the Mexican soldiers when they saw they had no uniforms or shoes, and their guns were so old they looked like antiques.

It was a time in history when Napoleon III, Emperor of France, saw an opportunity to build an empire in Mexico, which he considered weak. Mexico had lost over half of all its territory and Benito Juarez, Mexico's great President, had no money to pay Mexico's national debt to the European nations. Napoleon III planned to impose an emperor to govern all of Mexico. What he didn't count on was the will of the Mexican people not to be enslaved by a European power. The battle took place at PUEBLA, a city in Mexico.

General Zaragoza's unconventional battle tactics, the bravery of his army and the assistance he received from the citizens of Puebla were all important in defeating the French army. It is reported that women and children fought in the battle and used whatever weapons they had including pots and pans. In some cases women boiled water and threw it on the French army. The Mexican people gave the French a disastrous defeat by using their greatest weapons: their unity and their desire not to be enslaved.

Napoleon III had yet another plan for his army once it won the battle at Puebla. That plan was to continue marching to the United States to assist the southern states in their civil war against the North. Do you suppose history would have been different if General Lawrencez had not been defeated at Puebla? What if Napoleon III's plan to assist the South in their war against the North had worked?

People in Mexico and the United States celebrate Cinco de Mayo by throwing flowers at each other to re-create the battle at Puebla.

CINCO DE MAYO (seen-co   day   maee-yo)
IGNACIO ZARAGOZA (eeg-nahs-see-oh   sah-rah-goh-sah)
PUEBLA (poo-ay-blah)

GA1324

THE SIXTEENTH OF SEPTEMBER
PADRE MIGUEL HIDALGO Y COSTILLA

The Sixteenth of September is celebrated by Mexican Americans as another Fourth of July. Just as the Fourth of July is celebrated with speeches and parades to remind everyone of the defeat of the British and their king, the Sixteenth of September is remembered by Mexican Americans as the day when the Spanish and their king were overthrown. By the time of this War of Independence which began on September 16, 1810, Spain and its empire had ruled Mexico for three hundred years.

This special holiday is remembered as one in which a Spanish priest by the name of Father MIGUEL HIDALGO Y COSTILLA led a group of Indians in a war for the independence of Mexico. This war, which began in the town of Dolores, was fought because the Spanish rulers had become very repressive and were enslaving the native "indio" population. Among the social reforms, Father Hidalgo and his followers were seeking the abolition of slavery, doing away with the tribute that Indians had to pay and that Indians be allowed to cultivate the land for their own benefit.

Father Hidalgo did not live to see his dream realized; he was executed in May of 1811, but his ideas and those of his followers took hold and many years later the Spanish were defeated. With the death of Father Hidalgo and other important leaders like Father JOSE MARIA MORELOS, the movement for independence lost its most important leaders. Father Miguel Hidalgo y Costilla is known by all Mexicans as the Father of His Country.

MIGUEL HIDALGO Y COSTILLA (mee-goo-ayl ee-dahl-go ee cohs-tee-yah)
JOSE MARIA MORELOS (hoh-say mah-ree-ah moh-ray-los)

ANSWER KEY

54 Years and 600 Miles of Missions, page 3
1. San Diego de Acalá, 1769
2. San Carlos Borromeo de Carmelo, 1770
3. San Antonio de Padua, 1771
4. San Gabriel Arcángel, 1771
5. San Luis Obispo de Tolosa, 1772
6. San Francisco de Asís, 1776
7. San Juan Capistrano, 1776
8. Santa Clara de Asís, 1777
9. San Buenaventura, 1782
10. Santa Bárbara, 1786
11. La Purísima Concepción, 1787
12. Santa Cruz, 1791
13. Nuestra Señora de la Soledad, 1791
14. Santa José de Guadalupe, 1797
15. San Juan Bautista, 1797
16. San Miguel Arcángel, 1797
17. San Fernando Rey de España, 1797
18. San Luis Rey de Francia, 1798
19. Santa Inés, 1804
20. San Rafael Arcángel, 1817
21. San Francisco de Solano, 1823

California's Scenic Highway 1, page 4
3 Declarative
1 Interrogative
2 Exclamatory
4 Imperative
All other sentences in the reading are declarative.

Governors of California, page 6
1. José Joaquín de Arrillaga
2. Portolá, Romeu, Argüello
3. Echeandia, Alvarado
4. Sola, Victoria, Figueroa, Castro, Gutiérrez, Chico, Pico
5. Pablo Vicente Sola
6. high (upper) California
7. Baja (lower) California
8. Pio Pico

El Tratado, page 11
the United States—los Estados Unidos
article—articulo
the Mexican Republic—la República Mexicana
territories—territorios
the title and rights—el título y derechos
within one year—dentro de un año
citizens—ciudadanos
property—las propiedades

Animales, page 17
horse—caballo
camel—camello
animal—animal
deer—venado
rooster—gallo
snake—vibora
cat—gato
monkey—chango
pig—puerco
bird—pajaro
dog—perro
burro—burro

Organizing, page 29

1. MALDEF	1. AMAE
2. LULAC	2. LULAC
3. MAPA	3. MALDEF
4. AMAE	4. MAPA
5. UFW	5. UFW
6. NABE	6. NABE

Picking the Crops, page 32

ACROSS	DOWN
4. grapes	1. apple
6. olives	2. fig
7. peach	3. chives
8. raspberry	5. alfalfa
12. pomegranate	6. orange
15. lemon	9. wheat
16. lime	10. apricot
	11. walnuts
	13. almonds
	14. plum

"De Colores," page 33
1. campos—fields
2. primavera—spring
3. arco iris—rainbow
4. gallo—rooster
5. gallina—hen
6. pollitos—chicks
7. rooster—qui ri qui ri qui ri qui ri quí
8. hen—ca ra ca ra ca ra ca ra cá
9. chicken—pío pío pío pí

GA1324

Plays, page 37
1. *La Bamba*
2. *¡Bandido!*
3. *El Fin del Mundo*
4. *Corridos*
5. *Zoot Suit*
6. *Soldado Razo*
7. *I Don't Have to Show You No Stinking Badges!*

Teatros, page 39
1. Theater of the Farm Workers
2. Theater of the Cockroaches
3. Theater of the Neighborhood
4. Theater of Hope
5. Theater of the Spirit
6. Theater of the Earth
7. Theater of the Poor
8. Theater of the People
9. Our Theater
10. Theater of the Flea
11. Chili Pepper Theater

Canciones, page 45
1. "Two Little Trees"
2. "You, Only You"
3. "Let's Get Going"
4. "The Laurel Plants"
5. "Those Eyes"
6. "For a Love"
7. "The Big Cricket"
8. "The Rodeo"
9. "The Boat from Guaymas"
10. "You Are the Sun"

Music, page 49
Love Songs—Vikki Carr
Latin Rock and Roll—Trini Lopez
Folk Songs and Ballads—Joan Baez
Latin Jazz—Pete Escovedo
Mexican Trio Music—Pedro Gonzales, Jr.
Big Band Orchestras—Rafael Mendez
Texas Mexican Music—Lydia Mendoza
Rock and Roll—Richie Valens
Ballads and Corridos—Linda Ronstadt

Names, page 50
1. Florencia Martínez Cardona—Vikki Carr
2. Luis Antonio Alonso—Gilbert Roland
3. Antonio (Rudolfo Oaxaca) Quinn—Anthony Quinn
4. Ricardo Valenzuela—Richie Valens
5. Sheila Escovedo—Sheila E.

Who Painted the Picture? page 55
1. José Montoya
2. Manuel Unzueta
3. Manuel Neri
4. Malaquías Montoya
5. Alfredo Arreguín
6. Rupert Garcia

Books, page 66
1. And the Earth Did Not Part, Tomás Rivera
2. Rudolfo Acuña
3. Abelardo Barrientos Delgado
4. The Opinion, Ignacio E. Lozano, Sr.
5. Fifth Sun, Octavio Romano
6. Americo Paredes
7. Mexican American, José Antonio Villarreal
8. Rudolfo Anaya
9. Gary Soto

Accomplishments, page 71
1. Juan Gomez Quiñones
2. Tomás Arciniega
3. Cecilia Preciado de Burciaga
4. Julián Nava
5. Aturo Madrid Barela
6. Carlos Cortes
7. Frank Angel, Jr.
8. John Aragon
9. Carlos Castañeda
10. Julián Samora
11. Lauro Cavazos, Jr.

Sign Language, page 75
1. e.
2. d.
3. a.
4. c.
5. g.
6. b.
7. f.

Politician and Community Activist, page 78
Federal: regional director
State: assemblywoman
City: councilwoman

1973—President of Comisión Femenil de Los Angeles
1974—Administrative Assistant to Art Torres
1980—Chief Deputy to Willie Brown
1982—California State Assemblywoman
1983—*Caminos* magazine's Woman of the Year
1984—*MS.* magazine's Woman of the Year
1987—Los Angeles City Councilwoman

Champions, page 85
1. Tom Flores
2. Carlos Palomino
3. Danny Villanueva
4. Lee Treviño
5. Robert Chacon
6. Nancy Lopez
7. James Plunkett
8. Richard Alonso (Pancho) Gonzales

GA1324